WIDE-EYED AND LEGLESS

Jeff Connor was born in Manchester and now lives in Edinburgh. A freelance sportswriter, he has written 12 books, including the definitive story of the Busby Babes, *The Lost Babes*, and *Up and Down Under*, an account of the 2001 British Lions tour.

WIDE-EYED AND LEGLESS

INSIDE THE TOUR DE FRANCE

JEFF CONNOR

MAINSTREAM
PUBLISHING

EDINBURGH AND LONDON

This edition, 2011

First published in Great Britain by Simon & Schuster Ltd in 1988

This edition published in Great Britain in 2011 by
MAINSTREAM PUBLISHING COMPANY
(EDINBURGH) LTD
7 Albany Street
Edinburgh EH1 3UG

ISBN 9781845961718

A catalogue record for this book is available
from the British Library

Printed in Great Britain by
Clays Ltd St Ives plc

7 9 10 8 6

To My Father
ARTHUR CLIVE CONNOR

CONTENTS

Foreword by Richard Moore   9

Acknowledgements   13

Glossary   15

CHAPTER 1   Les Anglais   17

CHAPTER 2   Men at Work   31

CHAPTER 3   The Open Road   49

CHAPTER 4   Foul Play   64

CHAPTER 5   Tour de Farce   86

CHAPTER 6   The Big Boss   96

CHAPTER 7   The Irish Rovers   102

CHAPTER 8   And Some You Lose   113

CHAPTER 9   Golden Boy   132

CHAPTER 10   Far, Far the Mountain Peak   146

CHAPTER 11   Au Revoir   163

CHAPTER 12   The Next Horizon   172

Who Won What   176

Who Lost What   178

Who Was Who   180

Who Stayed Where   191

FOREWORD

In 2003, during a stint working on the sports desk at *Scotland on Sunday* newspaper, I was assigned a seat beside the paper's rugby correspondent. He was a fit-looking man in his early fifties with grey close-cropped hair, and for a couple of hours he sat talking on the phone, in dulcet northern tones, to various rugby people. It took about that long for the name – Jeff Connor – to register.

'*Wide-Eyed and Legless*?' I asked as he replaced the receiver after one call. It would have seemed an odd or impertinent question had I not suspected that the man sitting beside me might be the author of a book by this title. There was a brief pause before Connor smiled with what seemed a mixture of pleasure and surprise, thinking, mistakenly, that the book had been all but forgotten.

Au contraire. I told Connor how much I'd enjoyed his book and it became clear, as we talked, that it stoked some of his fondest sporting memories. He chuckled at the cast of remarkable, and in one or two cases bizarre, characters, including Phil Griffiths, Tony Capper, Malcolm Elliott, Adrian Timmis and Shane Sutton. Each had left the kind of impression that made a 16-year gap seem like 16 days. And as for the experience of his three weeks at the Tour de France, Connor had covered many major sporting events but nothing compared for scale, suffering, subterfuge, scandal and general insanity.

Few books capture that insanity as successfully as *Wide-Eyed and Legless*. I'd go further: Connor's account of the 1987 Tour is one of the most vivid and entertaining books ever written about the Tour de France.

Connor travelled to the start in West Berlin as an 'embedded' journalist with the first British professional team ever to be invited, ANC-Halfords. The team began in shambolic fashion and went downhill from there (not literally, sadly; they had the Pyrenees, Mont Ventoux and the Alps to tackle first).

Over the course of the three weeks the team unravelled. For Connor, who witnessed the unravelling at first hand, this was a stroke of incredible good fortune. In fact, it could hardly have worked out better – every mishap, setback and falling out was grist to his mill, and gold dust for his book.

As they suffered through the Pyrenees, toiled up Ventoux and laboured over the Alps, events just kept taking a turn for the worse – or, if you were Connor, for the better. Indeed, as the ANC-Halfords riders fell by the wayside, as the team's resources were stretched to breaking point and beyond, as tempers frayed and team owners abandoned, Connor's role changed. By the final week he was no longer an embedded journalist: he was a de facto member of the support staff. It offered him unparalleled access to the inner sanctum and a crash course in this exotic, strange sport, populated by *soigneurs*, *directeurs sportifs*, spivs, chancers, cheats and – last, and very often least – the athletes who pedal the 2,500 miles around France.

One of the most revealing things about *Wide-Eyed and Legless* is that it lays bare the status of the riders and their place in the pecking order. Though often described as 'Kings of the Road', in reality they were paupers, put up in dorm-style accommodation and afforded little in the way of luxury or comfort as they endured their daily struggle.

Almost a quarter of a century on, there are passages in Connor's book that read like a historical account, detailing aspects of the Tour and the sport that have disappeared or been phased out – though not as many as you might imagine. While riders no longer wash their own racing clothing, as they did in their hotel sinks in the 1980s, the Tour remains in many respects essentially the same, visiting the same places, watched by the same fans, run by the same people. The riders earn more money and arrive at stage starts in luxury buses, but they are still a long way from pampered footballers. Their lives are still defined by sacrifice and suffering (and, in some cases, drugs).

The ANC-Halfords story is an important one in the history of British cycling – and it serves as a cautionary tale. Their ambitious, larger-than-life owner, Tony Capper, overreached himself by impatiently pushing for the team to start the 1987 Tour. They had grown too fast, too quickly, and the team collapsed in financial disarray in the aftermath of their first and, as it turned out, only Tour.

This lends poignancy to the story contained in these pages, particularly when you reflect on the wasted potential. A rider like Adrian Timmis, for example, would surely have thrived had he been given the time to develop into the stage race rider he hinted at becoming in 1987. In another set-up Malcolm Elliott would have been a superstar – his performances in the 1987 Tour were remarkable in the circumstances. Indeed, Elliott was the only ANC-Halfords rider who went on to a successful career on the Continent; he made a comeback in his early forties and continued to race as a professional in Britain until 2010, on the eve of his 50th birthday. Elliott's class shone through in 1987, though he could, and should, have been the Mark Cavendish of his day.

As Shane Sutton – who, as Britain's head coach, has gone on to become one of the most influential figures in the British cycling success story of the past decade – told me in 2010: 'I was called up to ride the Tour at the last moment. I'd been ill since March and I was going to make up the numbers, which is not the way you should approach the Tour. We had talent in that team – Paul Watson, Graham Jones, Malcolm Elliott. But when someone of Graham's capabilities goes home early [Jones had ridden for top Continental teams and finished 20th in the 1981 Tour], you can see there was no morale. And for the ones who had families and mortgages, like myself, you just wanted to get home, get yourselves sorted out. You pin on a number in the morning but you're not thinking about the race.'

Twenty-three years later Sutton was one of the men at the helm of ANC-Halfords' successors, Team Sky. The second British professional team to enter the Tour – as Team Sky did in 2010 – was different in just about every imaginable way, certainly in terms of budget. And yet their tough baptism on the roads of France demonstrated that money cannot necessarily buy success and that – as ANC-Halfords also discovered in 1987 – there still appear to be cultural barriers to a British team conquering the sport of Continental cycling and its toughest event, the Tour de France. Unlike ANC-Halfords, Team Sky will at least be back for a second – and third, and fourth – crack. But the mind boggles when you think about the heights Elliott, Timmis, Watson, Jones et al. might have scaled had such a well-funded and well-organised team existed in the 1980s.

Connor may not have realised it at the time but, in *Wide-Eyed and Legless*, he was chronicling a significant story as well as anticipating the rising popularity of cycling and the Tour de France in Britain. This cycling zeitgeist is the catalyst for the long overdue re-publication of this classic book. But forget its significance or its place in the ever-expanding canon of cycling literature. More than anything, *Wide-Eyed and Legless*, with its cast of unforgettable heroes and villains, is entertaining. And, in places, bloody funny. Enjoy.

Richard Moore, London, 2011

ACKNOWLEDGEMENTS

SINCERE THANKS GO TO THE team and personnel of ANC-Halfords for their remarkable patience with and understanding of a cycling 'civilian' and to the other riders of the professional cycling fraternity – the greatest and bravest athletes in sport.

I would also like to offer appreciation to Phil Liggett of Channel 4 television for taking time from his busy schedule while in France to offer help and advice, and to Des Cahill of Radio Telefís Eireann for some memorable shared experiences on Tour.

Thanks go to Phil Griffiths, Phil O'Connor and Geoff Shergold for the photographs.

Finally, like the Tour de France, this book was a team effort and could not have been possible without the help of my wife Kath and my mother, Mrs Nancy Connor.

GLOSSARY

Bidon The plastic water bottle clipped on a rider's bike.

Break An escape by one or more riders from the main pack.

Bunch See '*Peloton*'.

Climber A usually lightweight rider employed for his ability in the mountains.

Commissaires The men who follow the race to enforce the rules.

Directeur sportif The team sports director, responsible for day-to-day running of the team plus tactics during a stage.

Domestiques The team's donkeys, there to supply their leader with refreshments, protect him in the pack and generally make his life easier. Literally 'servants'.

Flat A puncture.

Giro d'Italia The Italian version of the Tour de France, generally considered the second biggest prize in stage racing.

Milk Race The Tour of Britain, Britain's longest established stage race.

Musette The cotton tuck bag used to transfer food to riders on the move.

Neutralised zone The few kilometres out of the stage town to the official start.

Peloton The main pack of riders, in English 'the bunch'.

Prologue The time trial that traditionally precedes Stage 1 proper.

Radio Tour The short-wave race commentary broadcast from the race director's car and picked up by team vehicles and journalists.

Ravitaillement The feed half-way through a stage (sometimes two on longer stages).

Rouleur Literally a 'roller', but generally used to describe a cyclist at speed.

Route profile The cardboard cards carried in the jersey pocket which show villages, climbs, sprints, feed area and any difficulties en route.

Soigneur The French word describing a cycling team's masseur/dietician/counsellor/first aider.

Sprinter The team's specialist short-range speed merchants, always to the fore in massed finishes.

Stage A race within a race. On major tours the stages are generally town to town. The 1987 Tour had 25 stages varying in length from 20 miles to 170 miles.

Time limit Competitors can be eliminated if outside the stage time limit, a percentage of the winner's time depending on the severity of the stage.

Time triallist A time trial is a race against the clock over a set distance. It is the third of cycle racing's three traditional skills (climbing and sprinting are the others) and it tests the rider's ability to operate without team help.

Yellow jersey The traditional garb of the race leader.

CHAPTER 1

LES ANGLAIS

CYCLIST STEPHEN ROCHE RETURNED FROM the Continent to his Dundrum home on the outskirts of his native Dublin in June 1987 mentally and physically drained. He had just won the Giro d'Italia – the first part of cycling's great triumvirate which also includes the Tour de France and the World Championships in the same season – under the sort of circumstances that would have tried a saint.

In Italy he had been punched, spat upon and slandered by rabid Italian crowds. On some of the mountain stages they had held out slabs of red, raw meat at the roadside, indicating in their partisan way the fate they were wishing on Roche. An even more rabid Italian press railed daily at the little foreigner, and the management and most of his team mates on the Italian Carrera team had disowned him.

The catalyst for all this bile was the rivalry between Roche and his Carrera co-leader, the home favourite and defending champion, Roberto Visentini. Both Roche and the Italian believed they should win the Giro – Roche because he knew he was the better rider and Visentini because he was Italian and it was Italy's Tour.

When Roche ultimately took the pink jersey of race leader from Visentini against the orders of the Carrera management and held on to it through the last week of the 2,500-mile race it was safe to say that Roche was for a time the most-hated man in Italy.

To hang on to win under these circumstances indicated mental and physical fortitude of the highest order and many began to look to the 27-year-old Irishman to join cycling legends Fausto Coppi, Eddy Merckx, Jacques Anquetil and Bernard Hinault in the history books as men who have won the Giro and the Tour de France in the same year.

Roche himself wasn't so sure. On the Saturday night that the Giro ended he by-passed the Carrera celebration party and drove back to Paris wondering how much the efforts in Italy had taken out of him.

He had already determined that he wouldn't race before the Tour de France. Instead, while the press hunted for him, Roche slipped home to Ireland for a while before beginning his preparations for his tilt at cycling's greatest prize.

For Roche this meant relaxing, and the single-minded Dubliner had his own ideas on how to relax . . . pulling on a mechanic's overalls and tinkering with an old MG in his garage. He had 18 days before the Tour's prologue time trial in West Berlin.

While Roche whiled away his time deep in engine oil and axle grease, a 43-year-old millionaire businessman called Tony Capper was waiting anxiously in his Isle of Man home to hear if he, too, would be on the start line in Berlin. Capper, along with transport and haulage firm Associated Nationwide Couriers and the bicycle retailers Halfords, represented, as ANC-Halfords, the first British team challenge on the Tour in 20 years. They had paid their entry fee of £25,000, although the sponsorship costs of the full season, including the wages of staff, riders, transport and machinery, came closer to £600,000, and were now awaiting the final decision from the Société du Tour de France.

Capper, at first sight, looks an unlikely figure to be involved in sport. At 20 stone plus, a dedicated chain smoker and in his own words 'not wearing very well', Capper is a rough diamond who made his fortune when he founded and then sold out ANC.

Born and brought up the son of a miner in Stoke-on-Trent, Capper had had a chequered and mystery-shrouded career, joining the Army at sixteen, leaving six years later to become what he described as 'a very tolerant policeman' and later running a taxi business in Stoke.

'I had eight years in the police force,' he says. 'But rather than report someone for an offence I'd spend an hour bending their ear and convincing them what they were doing was wrong. If you can illustrate things to people it's easier to convince them. I used to actually enjoy this and perhaps I'd rather let them off than nick them. There were that many people around doing things wrong anyway that you could miss twenty-five of them by trying to catch one.

'But I admit I went off my beat. I stood there and said, yes, what I did was wrong. You should be on one side of the street or the other and if you cross to the other side of the street you're in the wrong.'

Capper left the police force with two months' pay and a car, but his first taxi business ended in disaster.

'It ended up as a very sad tale really because I got involved with another guy who lived next door to me and we ended up splitting up. He was a bit too young and inexperienced and he committed suicide.'

Capper founded ANC as an overnight express delivery service in 1981. At one time in the company's early days Capper admits that he had liabilities of around £200,000, but one thing you could say about Capper is that he never panics. In five years he built the business into a profitable enterprise until British and Commonwealth Shipping bought him out in 1986. Capper, however, didn't let go completely.

While chairman of the company he had dabbled in darts, football and athletics as promotional outlets before settling on professional cycling road racing.

To Capper there was nothing to match the sport in terms of media coverage per pound spent. He could see the name ANC on British and European TV, splashed all over the national and regional press and talked of in the same breath abroad as the great cycling outfits of Système U, Carrera or Kas.

Capper, of course, also saw the possibilities for himself. A supreme opportunist, he had made himself believe that one day he would control the purse strings of a cycling team containing a Tour de France yellow jersey or, at the very least, a stage winner. There was also the basic and undeniably egotistical, not to mention schoolboyish, delight of motoring around the Continent in charge of a major cycling team, athletes whose fates and fortunes rested with him. And, as Capper liked to put it as he scattered pedestrians on the way through a town or made a U-turn across the central reservation of a dual carriageway, being inside an official Tour Peugeot was 'as good as being in the presidential limousine'.

Capper and ANC, as well as dominating domestic cycling and winning the 1987 Tour of Britain Milk Race, had cut their teeth in a number of the early-season European classics and Capper could at least claim he had assembled the strongest and most successful British team available, although in his final Tour line-up only four of the nine riders were British born.

In stage races like the Tour de France the team element is vital and the composition of that team is largely based on the varying terrain and the difficulties ahead.

Most teams have designated leaders whose aim is the yellow jersey of Tour victor and much of the teamwork revolves around giving the superstar as comfortable a time as possible, an armchair ride with everything concentrated on the ultimate victory bid.

That's why a team manager will surround his main man with *'domestiques'* – literally 'servants' – whose job is to pamper the leader, fetching and carrying his food and drink from the team car during a stage and, if possible, keeping him wrapped up in a vacuum of their own creation away from the wind on the road. It's the same principle as the recreational rider pedalling in the slipstream of a bus on the way to work – it is so much easier when someone else is making all the effort.

On the road during a stage, the main tactics of *domestiques* are to keep the tempo high so that no one can attack their man by breaking away off the front of the main pack, or to work together to chase down any dangerous breaks. That's why so often in the closing 20 or 30 miles of a stage you will see the same team jerseys alternating the lead at the front, each taking a spell of effort before drifting back to make way for a team mate. Of course, other teams may not be too happy about all this – particularly if one of their men has broken away and is being pursued – so they will do their utmost to break up the rhythm of the chase by forcing their way into one of the relays and then deliberately slowing down.

Nowadays, every team leader is a marked man and it's virtually impossible for him to get clean away for a stage win, so a shrewd team manager will also have a couple of up-and-coming riders capable of some minor adventures in their own right and perhaps a stage win or a brief spell as race leader. As relative unknowns their moves off the front of the main pack are liable to be allowed more leeway by other teams.

The main disciplines of cycling are sprinting, time trialling and climbing, each requiring quite different effort and approach. All teams have their specialists, but inevitably it's the man who can do all three consistently better than everyone else who wins the Tour de France.

The sprinters are inevitably big men capable of turning a big gear at speed and able to use elbows and arms to look after themselves in the mayhem of a bunch sprint. On flat stages they will be cossetted deep in the pack, preserving their energies until the time comes when one or two team mates will lead them towards a good position at the front (with perhaps a couple more on his rear wheel to prevent anyone slipstreaming). In the last few kilometres the tactical jockeying will begin until the bit players move aside and all that is left are the high-speed supermen and their final swaying, snarling charge towards the line.

The climbers are less gregarious in their approach and tend to be introverted types used to their lonely battles. With the pace at 13–15 miles per hour on major climbs there is no sheltering on the windward side of a team mate, which is why on most climbs the pack will break apart like an exploding grenade. The favoured tactic of a specialist climber is to have a team mate keep the tempo high so that no one can jump away. Roche invariably had his personal *domestique* perform this function for him, and on the one occasion that he failed, the Irishman swiftly recruited members of other teams to do the same job. Ultimately, however, a climber must have the very special physical and mental make-up that will allow him to travel up and around 10 per cent Alpine gradients as if on a smoothly moving escalator.

Tour winners are inevitably good time triallists because in the race against the clock it comes down to pure solo effort. With no team mates to help, the time triallist has to reach within himself for the effort to keep turning a big gear unwaveringly for mile after mile. It's here, too, where economy of effort will count and why a stylist like Roche will always come to the fore.

It has to be said, ANC did not possess an ultimate winner and the complicated tactical nuances of many of the other teams were not necessary.

ANC's team leader was **Malcolm Elliott**, the 26-year-old Milk Race winner and the glamour boy of British cycling. Elliott is a plain-speaking Yorkshireman from Sheffield around whom Capper was building most of his hopes. Elliott had turned professional at the end of 1983 and his 1987 season had included a third place in the Amstel Gold Classic in Holland in April, a race which ultimately only got away because of the all-Dutch alliance of the first and second men. Elliott's blond good looks and carefully nurtured suntan, plus a high-powered Porsche, had given him an unfortunate playboy image, but through this and his domestic successes he had remained level-headed and indeed self-effacing.

A two-year spell in France as an amateur had made him more worldly and approachable than his colleagues, although at times his native bluntness made him difficult. Elliott, it could be said, did not suffer fools gladly. When I asked him before the Tour if this was the peak of his career, he had replied with ill-concealed scorn: 'Why, is it all downhill after this?'

Adrian Timmis had celebrated his 23rd birthday 10 days before the Tour started. At 5 ft 9 in. and 10 stone, Timmis off the bike looks like a fresh-faced schoolboy, an impression reinforced by an almost painful shyness. In fact that shyness masks remarkable determination and considerable courage. Timmis is a man who doesn't believe in wasted effort – everything, including talking, comes second to his ambition of becoming a major cycling talent. Exposed to his first Tour de France, Timmis changed almost visibly during the month in France, from a gawky young boy to a mature professional cyclist.

Graham Jones is one of Britain's best-ever cyclists and easily the most experienced on the team, having placed 20th in the 1981 Tour. At 30 Jones was close to the end of a distinguished career that had included the amateur points championship of France in 1978 and a lengthy spell with Peugeot's famous 'Foreign Legion' team of professional cyclists. Quiet and self-contained most of the time, Jones in his role as team elder statesman, and perhaps able to see more than most the way things should have gone, was often critical of the ANC organisation. Unfairly maybe, the management labelled him the team's 'barrack-room lawyer'.

Paul Watson was the team's climbing hope, a chirpy 25-year-old from Milton Keynes with a bleached-blond haircut, earring and a definite eye for a pretty face. As guardians of the team's morals, Capper and his management were plagued continually by the thought that Watson was dedicating more of himself to his girlfriends than to the team.

Shane Sutton was the team's character, an Australian from Moree near Sydney who had arrived in Britain in 1984 and made an immediate impact with his performances in the Kelloggs city-centre road races. Shane had the reputation of a boozer and a brawler but having slimmed down from a one-time 11 stone to his racing weight of 10 and settled into a marriage and mortgage in Rowley Regis, West Midlands, he had shown enough consistency and speedy finishing to earn a place in the Tour team. Sutton's good humour made him enjoyable company at most times, although his Tour was to become a long-drawn-out struggle for survival that stretched that humour to the limit.

Steve Swart is a blond New Zealander with the quiet adaptability, nomadic nature and determination of the true Kiwi. Swart had landed in Britain from Hamilton in 1986 looking for a professional contract and with ANC-Halfords finished sixth in the 1987 Milk Race. Like Sutton, Swart's race was to turn into an extended and heroic battle with pain.

Kvetoslav Palov, known as Omar to his team mates for reasons of brevity, is a mournful 25-year-old Czech who, after defecting from his national team in June 1986 on the way home from a racing trip to Italy, found himself first in Germany then in Australia where he took out citizenship.

In April 1987 Palov arrived in Britain, struck up a friendship with Malcolm Elliott in Sheffield, signed professional forms with ANC and within three months was in the world's greatest cycling race. At times Palov wore the look of a man who couldn't believe it had all happened to him so quickly. But Palov was a fine athlete and turned out to be one of the team's strong men, completing the Tour with something to spare.

ANC, for reasons not unconnected with winning final approval from the Tour selection committee, also had two French members.

Guy Gallopin is president of the French Federation of Cyclists and at 31, with five Tours behind him, a pillar of experience. Gallopin is the archetypal hard man, a former gymnast with a black belt in judo. 'He'd make a good miner,' Capper said of him admiringly in the ultimate tribute of a miner's son. Gallopin, despite his lack of English, was also the friendliest and most approachable man in the team.

Bernard Chesneau was born in Blois in the Loire Valley. At 27 and in his third year as a professional, 'Ches' was plagued by bronchitis and struggled almost from the first day. He departed, inconsolable, before the Tour even reached French soil. Ill as he was, the Frenchman's pride hurt a lot more.

Gone are the days when Tour riders had to change their own tyres and repair their own punctures. Behind the modern professional cyclist is a formidable line-up of trained staff. Basically 'all' a rider has to do is pedal, eat and rest, all other functions being taken care of by personnel who ensure that they are woken each day on time, fed with the right foods, dressed in the correct clothing and mounted on the correct machinery, driven to and from the stage start, fed en route, have their bikes serviced on the road and advised on tactics during the race.

At the finish line they are transported to their respective hotels, fed and massaged and have their wounds and ailments attended to. On the face of it more pampered sportsmen it would be hard to find . . . until you realise what a brutalising and hazardous experience a day's work can become.

Besides Capper (the team manager), ANC's back-up consisted of a Paris-based businessman with the title of 'press relations officer', **Donald Fisher**, although his exact function never became clear apart from providing Capper with instant French-to-English translations of the race commentary in the team car. Fisher always claimed he was born in Scotland but the accent was more Maurice Chevalier than Harry Lauder.

The joint team directors – the *directeurs sportifs* – and the men responsible for the day-to-day running of the team including stage tactics, were **Edouard** ('Ward') **Woutters**, a crusty middle-aged Belgian who lasted one week, and **Phil Griffiths**, a fast-talking salesman from Stoke who took over.

Woutters, who works for the Belgian water board, was an experienced Continental *directeur sportif*, but ANC and Capper had only agreed to his participation as part of a deal with one of their sponsors, drinks manufacturers Tonnis-steiner, who had agreed to fund the team's vehicles for a season . . . as long as Ward went with them. Like every other member of the management this was Ward's first Tour de France.

Griffiths was a highly successful amateur rider before taking up team administration. A canny and knowledgeable *directeur sportif*, Griffiths, after Ward's departure, nevertheless found himself relegated to the second, back-up car while Capper and Fisher swaggered up and down in the lead car. Griffiths at times found this hard to take.

No one could ever come up with a satisfactory translation of the French *soigneur* but Capper's description of them as 'witch doctors' seems close enough. Suffice to say that the *soigneurs* look after the riders' bodies and minds, preparing their specific high-energy foods, giving massage and helping with the driving. The *chef soigneur* of the team was **Angus Fraser**, a large scar-faced Scot from Linlithgow, who as a sports therapist numbers sprinter Allan Wells among his clients. For business reasons Fraser arrived late and left early but his formidable presence left no one in doubt that he outranked Belgian **Roger Van der Vloet**, who left with Woutters after one week, German **Friedhelm Steinborn** and Frenchman **Sabino Pignatelli**. There were problems in communication between not only riders and *soigneurs* but also *soigneur* and *soigneur*.

Roger spoke mainly Flemish with a smattering of French, while Friedhelm, a huge and genial pot-bellied German from Cologne, spoke only German. Sabino, at 22, was the youngest of the party and had only French. Because of his age and diminutive stature Sabino became the team whipping boy, the convenient one to blame when things went wrong, which they frequently did. It became fashionable to swear and curse at little Sabino at length in English knowing he couldn't understand a word. Like a dog, however, Pignatelli would usually pick up the tone of the conversation.

Perhaps the hardest-worked men in the team were the mechanics, who frequently toiled a 15-hour day, adjusting each individual's bike in the morning for the demands of the day's ups and downs, diving out with handfuls of wheels when a rider punctured during a stage and washing the mud – and sometimes the blood – from the bikes at the night's overnight stop.

Chief mechanic, and Britain's only full-time one, was **Steve Snowling**, a well-known character in Britain and on the Continent. Backing him were **Steve Taylor** and **Geoff Shergold**, while **Nick Rawling** appeared from Britain to replace Shergold when he had to return to work in Britain.

* * *

With so many men doing so many separate tasks, each little group – the riders, the management, the *soigneurs* and the mechanics – believed that they had the most important job, a situation which led to the development of cliques who guarded each other's rights and territories absolutely.

Completely apart from these factions was the author, a 41-year-old sports journalist with the *Star* newspaper, there at the invitation of ANC-Halfords but sent by my sports editor in the belief that I would be able to ride a stage in the Tour and tell the *Star* readers what it was like, though I hadn't been on a bicycle since my youth.

Not surprisingly, this intrusion into the private and very esoteric world of a cycling team didn't find complete favour, although I did my best to stay out of the way and keep quiet. As I liked to point out from time to time to Phil Griffiths: 'You could have been lumbered with a real tabloid journalist pig.'

And as Griffiths liked to point out in his turn: 'If you had been a real pig we'd have bombed you out.'

In the end, the ANC team became so strapped for personnel that I found myself first driving the Citroën turbo estate carrying the *soigneurs*' gear to the hotel each day and then being entrusted with the team's battered and unroadworthy Iveco van, containing not only the riders' suitcases but also thousands of pounds' worth of expensive cycling equipment.

That van and driver didn't disappear over a mountain hairpin on more than one occasion owes more to good luck than good driving.

This, then, was the uneasy cosmopolitan and regional mix, the disparate bunch of personalities and temperaments who were to take on the most punishing marathon in sport.

The nine riders left home, if not exactly with the eyes and hopes of the nation upon them, at least with the expectation that Britain's first trade team in 20 years would not disgrace themselves.

At the lowest level of optimism it was hoped most of the riders would enter Paris in one piece after the month-long 2,600-mile thrash through France in mid summer. Rasher forecasts, mainly from Capper and the team sponsors, had predicted a top-20 finish for an ANC rider or even a stage win. Some critics on the other hand forecast a complete disaster, with the French mocking the pathetic efforts of 'les Anglais' as they strove to compete in a sport foreign to them.

Some of the most damning indictments of the ANC expedition came from former British professionals. One of them, Barry Hoban, winner of several Tour de France stages, summed up accurately when he said: 'Most of the British team have not seen a real mountain where a rider can lose a minute for each kilometre he climbs. I am not slating them. I would love the team to do well but their entry is premature. Maturity and experience are main factors and they are missing and that goes for the team management, too.

'The race is not just at the front. There is a daily struggle not to be eliminated by finishing outside the deadline. I hope the lads don't get hammered too much, because many riders have been ruined by the Tour. I just hope they all finish and prove me wrong.'

In the end, when the whole vast cavalcade of riders, team cars, team buses, publicity vehicles and press and photographers drove onto the Champs-Elysées there were but four survivors in the ANC team. The others had fallen by the wayside in various degrees of pain, embarrassment and relief. The five riders who didn't make it could console themselves that neither did the team manager and number one *directeur sportif*, nor did 67 other riders of various nationalities.

Between the high hopes and nervous wonderment of West Berlin and the anti-climactic exhaustion of the ending 26 days later in

Paris lies a story of heroism and amazing physical effort, of bravery to the point of folly, of commercial manipulation and of cynical rule-bending, which in any other professional game would be classed as cheating. All in the cause of the Great Race, the Tour de France.

CHAPTER 2

MEN AT WORK

IN TERMS OF HEART AND lung efficiency professional cyclists have always scored consistently ahead of other top-class athletes like marathon runners. Along with cross-country skiers they are quite simply the fittest men in sport. On dry land and away from their bikes, however, they certainly don't look it.

It would have taken a perceptive traveller to have noticed something unusual about the group gathered in the departure lounge at Heathrow on June 29 1987 Flight BA774 to West Berlin. On the surface they looked like a normal bunch of bachelors heading for the sun, clad in shorts or tracksuit bottoms and T-shirts or vests, wandering round the airport shops or chatting animatedly.

But these particular tourists all walked in a slow, flatfooted, energy-saving shuffle on shaven shapely legs like those of young athletic girls. Most had deep suntans and hadn't yet left the sodden English summer of 1987 behind, suntans that ended halfway up the arms and thigh.

Above all they ate. They'd eaten on the way down from the headquarters of Action Sports, Capper's cycling management company in the back streets of Stoke; they'd eaten at the motorway services halfway down the M1 and were eating as they waited for the flight. It didn't take long to realise that to be a champion cyclist you must be a champion eater, too. Food – the right kind of it – is fuel. Elliott admitted that at times he ate until it hurt, and to see 10-stone Adrian Timmis at the daily breakfast could be quite alarming.

Little wonder then that, as well as the peculiar, penguin-like walks and the muscular development that ends above the legs, most of the 207 riders in the Tour before a stage had the swollen upper abdomens of men who had deliberately overfilled their bellies.

The day had begun in the sort of organised chaos that was to characterise ANC's Tour de France. Griffiths (the joint team director), Graham Jones (who shook hands left-handed – he had a sandwich in the right) and Steve Swart were still loading bikes, wheels and clothing onto the team cars in Stoke four hours before we were due to depart from Heathrow. Elliott failed to turn up at the pre-arranged meeting point, driving straight down to the airport in a spare team car alone.

I introduced myself to Timmis, who shook hands shyly then moved away as quickly as possible, but Elliott at the airport was more effusive, posing for photographs by the *Star* photographer and dazzling the air hostesses with his flashing smile, emerald-green vest and suntan, the only tan on the team that stretched past the point normally covered by a short-sleeved cycling jersey. Shane Sutton the Aussie was proudly showing off his skinhead haircut and cracking jokes, while Watson, recalling the team's responsibilities to their employers, was wondering if they shouldn't have worn something with the sponsors' names on for the official photographs. Swart was busy helping to wrap the riders' bicycles carefully in polythene for loading into the Boeing 737 cargo hold. Adrian was eating again.

Capper, who hates flying, arrived at the last minute. It wasn't until the engines had begun revving that we saw his huge bulk squeezing down the aisle towards what turned out – to his horror – to be a no-smoking seat.

'Hey, Shane, here's Fatman,' said Jones with what seemed at the time to be unseemly disrespect as Capper loomed into view, resembling in his vast wheezing bulk the actor Sidney Greenstreet.

'Afternoon, boss,' called Shane. 'You just made it.'

'Bloody hell, couldn't you have found me a smoker?' grumbled the team manager as he ambled towards the rear of the plane in an effort to find an empty seat in the permitted smoking zone.

The flight passed in a stream of wisecracks from Shane. To his delight he found a magazine article on the Tour and the ANC team that described Graham Jones as 'a veteran cyclist' and took great delight in pointing this out to Graham. Graham was not amused.

Shane then turned on me. 'Hey, Jeff, what did you think of that Starbird Beverley on the Milk Race?'

The *Star* had been involved in the promotion of the Milk Race, which was won by Malcolm Elliott with Paul Watson as King of the Mountains, and daily pictures of the famous Beverley posing with the stage winners had landed on my desk.

'So so,' I replied.

'Hey, Paul,' roared Shane in delight at Watson, 'have you heard what he thinks about your sister?'

The flight was half empty, which to the delight of the riders meant they could have two dinners each, although all carefully avoided coffee, as caffeine at high levels is a banned drug and cyclists have to carefully maintain the amount in their bloodstream at the permitted 'allowance'.

Berlin was hot and stuffy even at 7 pm and it was a relief to be picked up by joint team director Ward Woutters and the Belgian *soigneur* Roger and drive out to the airport hotel in two of the official Peugeots supplied by the Société du Tour de France.

Steve Snowling, Steve Taylor and Geoff Shergold, the mechanics, were already at work building wheels and checking frames when we arrived, a scenario to be repeated daily over the next month – while the riders ate and rested, the mechanics worked.

Berlin Airport's Novotel was in many ways the ideal stopover for a cycling team. There was room for the mechanics to spread over the grass and a plentiful and easily attainable supply of water for washing bikes, large rooms for the *soigneurs* and their massage tables, and private dining areas for the riders to gorge in peace and for the management to talk tactics and build some team spirit.

The essential for all sporting teams on the road, whether it be cricket, basketball or cycling, is a closely bonded and sometimes artificially created togetherness, so Capper and Woutters were far from happy when Steve Taylor, having finished his stint on the bikes, appeared for his late dinner and sat amongst the riders who were just finishing off.

'I don't want to see that again,' said Capper. 'When a rider looks up from his dinner all I want him to see is a team mate. I know we're in the dark about this Tour and every day is going to be different. We're going to be pissed around – a lot. But this team's going to do things right.' Capper sat down, his first and last pep talk over.

Chesneau and Gallopin, the two Frenchmen, sat there with blank faces. They hadn't understood a word. Sutton and Watson, the two team comedians, laughed and joked their way through Capper's speech, while Elliott and Timmis just got on with the eating. Omar Palov, the Czech, sat almost comatose in thought and it suddenly struck me that Berlin was probably the worst place in the West for a defector from the Communist system. The thought of a snatch squad coming over the Wall and taking him back must have loomed large. Palov would surely have chosen any other place on earth to start his first Tour de France.

Meal times on Tour were extraordinary affairs with everything subordinated to the necessity of getting as much food as quickly as possible inside the riders. This meant a reprimand for the waiters who came in and started serving Fisher first and I was soon to become immune to the initially surprising sight of Sutton or Timmis wandering over to our table and helping themselves to anything that took their fancy.

The management also had an early forewarning that Watson's mind wasn't completely concentrated on the demands of cycling when a vivacious brunette walked unannounced into the ANC dining room asking for 'Paul'.

'Disgraceful,' said Fisher in the bar later that night after the riders had been packed off to bed. 'Girls do not belong on the Tour de France.'

Roger snorted in contemptuous surprise: '*Non, non*, Anquetil he won five Tours on champagne and that' – the Belgian held his forefinger in the air and wiggled it graphically – 'women never did him any harm.'

'But it's wrong, it will affect his performance.'

'My friend,' advised Roger, 'you have a lot to learn about *cyclisme*.'

Fisher wasn't the only one with a lot to learn. At dinner I had mentioned to Ward that my newspaper wanted me to interview Robert Millar, the Scot riding for the Dutch Panasonic team who were staying in the same hotel. I'd asked Woutters when was the best time to approach a rider, or should I ask the team manager first? Millar had a reputation for being difficult. Ward was all business.

'You want to interview Millar? Wait there.' Before I could stop him, the Belgian *directeur sportif* strode off towards the Panasonics dining room. Within two minutes he was back, red-faced and a little puzzled.

'Did you see Millar?' I asked.

'Yes, I saw Peter Post the Panasonics manager who is a friend of mine. They are eating but Post waves me to sit down. Millar is very angry and sent a message to you.'

'Yes?' I asked expectantly.

'Millar said: "Tell the journalist to fuck off."'

'That sounds like Millar,' said Phil Liggett, the Channel 4 TV commentator, when I retold him the story. 'He's been really awkward with us in the past. Personally I think it's a disgrace. He has a duty to his sponsor to represent the team and you don't do that by telling journalists to fuck off. Dinner time was a bad time to tackle him anyway. The best time is before the start of a stage before they register. If they don't want to talk they'll just ride away.'

Capper had a different theory.

'He hates us being here. He hates looking at us because it reminds him of home and he hates Glasgow and Britain. They tried to make him a freeman and he wouldn't even turn up for the ceremony. He doesn't even want to talk in English any more.'

West Berlin had paid £1 million for the honour of staging the start of the Tour de France. The logistics of transferring 23 teams and 207 riders created unwanted headaches for the individual team managers and *directeurs sportifs*, but there was little doubt that the city saw the Tour off in style, although with some inevitable hiccups. The prologue, a 4-mile individual time trial up and down the notorious Kurfürstendamm, was scheduled for July 1, with Stage 1 on the following day bracketed with a team time trial.

But first we had one spare non-racing day, or perhaps not so spare day since the riders had to undergo medicals and get some much-needed training in, while the *directeurs sportifs* organised team cars, supervised the preparation of the time trial bikes, received the draw for the time trial along with route profiles and maps for the whole Tour.

For the press, it was time for accreditation and to go in search of the valuable little green card, the passport to the inner workings of the Tour for which a cycling fan would give his right arm.

Underneath the sign saying 'Chefs de Presse' in the huge entrance hall of Berlin's Palais am Funkturm the father-and-son team of Claude and Philippe Sudres were holding court. The Sudres headed a 20-strong secretariat responsible for catering to the demands of the 800 or so press and TV people. Telephones, telex machines and a formidable team of middle-aged lady telephonists preceded the Tour on its daily journey, and journalists would arrive each evening at the host town for the next day's stage to find everything set up to cope with the demands of communicating with the world. Father Claude wore a red bandana around his neck and the carefully nurtured moustache of an ageing roué and greeted each old friend with an effusive hug. Having queued and sweated for ten minutes in his line I was a bit disgruntled to find that Claude didn't have much time for 'les Anglais', especially Englishmen he didn't know, and waved me dismissively over to Philippe's lengthening queue.

I wasn't the only one in difficulty. Des Cahill, a young Irishman from Radio Telefis Eireann who had followed Stephen Roche's Tour of Italy, was also having trouble with Claude. In the same mentality of squaddies in a barracks under the lash of a bullying sergeant major we had soon joined forces to tackle the myriad of problems that beset Tour rookies.

Ward Woutters and Capper, meanwhile, having overseen the pasting of the ANC-Halfords logos on the two official team cars and the brake provided and collected the Tour maps and stage cards, were also experiencing some difficulty.

Ward had arrived with the nine riders too early for the medical and this hadn't gone down too well with them, particularly the experienced Graham Jones.

Graham appeared completely out of sorts. For a start, the day's training hadn't gone well. With no one knowing the area around the airport a local girl had led the nine riders out and about on to the stifling, stuffy, fume-choked roads.

'It's a terrible place to train,' said Jones in disgust as he arrived back with the others, red-faced and sweating.

In contrast, Luis Herrera, the leader of the Café de Colombia team from South America, showed what an advantage he and his countrymen had in hot weather. Herrera, who away from his bike resembles a little bird but on it is arguably the best climber in the sport, had just finished a training spin, too, but not a bead of perspiration was visible as he went back to his room for massage.

Jones had complained to Woutters about the wait for the medical and Woutters was fuming as he drove back.

'The British team is not professional,' said the outspoken Belgian. 'They have to learn patience. It wasn't my fault about the medical but Graham Jones felt he had to complain. When the Tour starts we'll see where he is; there are better riders in Britain than him. The Milk Race – that's nothing, an amateur event. This is THE Tour. They call Paul Watson a climber because they saw him go up one steep hill but the Tour is about col after col. Malcolm Elliott – a playboy. He's a tremendous talent but he doesn't know how to suffer. I don't think he will make Paris. Sutton is not good enough for the Tour – I wanted [Chris] Lillywhite.'

As we swung into the hotel car park I asked Ward if he rated anyone in the ANC team.

'Yes, Adrian Timmis is a great talent. He can get into the top 20 on this Tour. He has the most tremendous powers of recuperation. Swart and Palov I know nothing about, but Gallopin will finish in Paris. He knows that art.' We were two days into the

Tour de France and the *directeur sportif* of ANC-Halfords had just written most of his team off.

The Tour organisers handed ANC an enormous publicity coup – Ward always claimed that he had arranged it – when Shane Sutton was drawn as the first rider away in the prologue time trial. Not so good for Shane, of course, as he'd have no one in front to chase, no 'minute man' as they call him in the trade when the riders go off at 60-second intervals. Cycling knows the time trial as the 'race of truth' – no team work, no hiding in a pack, just one rider against the clock. Past Tours have invariably been decided on time trial ability, although the prologue, at 4 miles, was nothing more, metaphorically speaking, than someone blowing a whistle to get the whole race going.

By night the Kurfürstendamm is a mess of prostitutes, drug addicts and drop-outs but on the morning of July 1 it was a vibrant 2-mile-long festival of light and noise with one end of the street blocked by waiting team cars – all with the individual riders' names pasted across a board on the front fender – the riders warming up in their multi-coloured, sponsor-spattered jerseys and the Berliners appearing in their thousands to see the start. In all it was estimated that three million West Germans watched the Tour in its four days of racing there, and with much of the action taking place in the British and American sectors of Berlin there was plenty of support for ANC.

The team's Tour, in fact, had almost come to a premature end the night before.

Much to the riders' annoyance, having trained, eaten and had massage, they had to don their cycling gear again and do their bits for TV at an opening-night show in front of an invited audience of personalities and local politicians.

We had been following a German police motor cyclist in one of the team cars, the bicycles stacked on top, when he had driven

39

down an underpass only eight feet high. Only Ward's quick braking prevented us following and wiping out several thousand pounds' worth of racing equipment.

So there, safely, was Shane at 11 am on the Kurfürstendamm in the shadow of the bombed church, swallowing nervously in the tiny glass-sided caravan in which each rider waits before a time trial. Behind the little Australian was a line of other riders awaiting their turn. In front was the sloping ramp leading down on to the road and a narrow corridor of crowd.

At last the clock ticked down its final 30 seconds, Shane breathed sharply in and out, then swished away to a huge roar. The 74th Tour de France was under way.

It wasn't a good trial for Sutton, as he was almost caught by the second man off – a real humiliation in a time trial as short as this – the giant raw-boned Czech Milan Jurco.

Coming down the finishing straight the two riders made a comical sight, with 5 ft 8 in. Shane being run down by the 6 ft 1 in. Jurco, like a bear pursuing a rabbit. Shane held him off . . . just . . . and for all of five seconds he and ANC led the Tour.

The cycling world's superstars went towards the end and they were feted like film stars as they approached the start, most of them moving slowly under a mass of notebooks and microphones.

'Stephen, have you recovered from Italy?'

'Sean, have you recovered from Spain?'

'*Comment ça va, Laurent?*'

'Good luck, Stephen.'

'*Bonne chance, Laurent.*'

Ward had given me permission to follow one of the ANC riders, and eventually I climbed into the car carrying the name of Graham Jones.

The tension mounted as Ward revved his engine, Jones was

shoved down the ramp and the Peugeot accelerated after him.

Ward was unimpressed. With the speedometer hovering at around 45 kilometres per hour he gestured resignedly, first at the clock and then at Jones straining away in front.

'Finished,' he said. 'Jones used to be a good *rouleur*, now, nothing.'

It seemed a harsh judgement on a man who had been one of Britain's better professionals.

As Woutters spoke, the road at the turning point at just past 2 miles rose slightly and Jones climbed out of the saddle so that he wouldn't have to change down a gear. As we turned and set off down the other side of the street, another rider was approaching fast in the opposite direction accompanied by a huge Germanic roar. I pointed him out to Woutters.

'That's Thurau,' he said, nodding appreciatively towards the local German hero in the colours of the Belgian Roland-Skala team.

'Look at him, there's an example of a good *rouleur*. He pedals easily, no wobbling, his torso's straight and his head doesn't move.'

Looking up ahead again at Graham Jones I couldn't help notice the rolling shoulders, the head moving from side to side and the wobbling wheels.

Stephen Roche, one of the Tour's hot favourites, had finished third in the prologue and it was soon clear that while his name meant a lot to his fellow Irishmen his face and lifestyle were not as yet so familiar. At least not in Berlin.

That night Des Cahill and I, after much searching, managed to find an Irish bar in the basement of a huge shopping centre and the barman, a fresh-faced, black-haired and earnest youngster of the type who colonise the best hotels in Dublin, quickly ran down Des's accent.

'Are you from Dublin?' he asked.

It was past midnight and Des was in the process of adding a few more ounces to his 14-stone frame with a large pint of stout. I couldn't resist it.

'Yeah, this is Stephen Roche,' I said.

'Stephen,' cried the astonished barman, 'I didn't recognise you without your cycling clothes on!'

Berlin's Brandenburg Gate was the official start for Stage 1. The grim lookout towers and machine guns of the Wall overshadowed the colourful cavalcade that assembled for the 67 miles around the city suburbs.

Malcolm Elliott showed evidence of good form by placing 17th for ANC in a race won by Nico Verhoeven of the Dutch Super Confex team 23 seconds ahead, and the Yorkshireman was still going well in the afternoon's team time trial through the British sector.

But for one team the day turned into a disaster and demonstrated that the Germans' much vaunted organisation did have a few flaws. A police motor cyclist outrider lost his way, taking the Spanish team BH down the wrong street and losing them 2 minutes. The BH riders reappeared on the right road with much fist shaking and swearing and to sympathetic applause, but I couldn't help wondering what would have happened if it had been one of the French, or Roche's Carrera team that had been led astray. The Irish favourite's Tour could have been lost on only its second day. Or would they have asked for a re-run?

The long finishing straight of Martin Luther King Strasse leading down to the John F. Kennedy Platz was an ideal viewpoint as the riders wound up for the last effort, alternating leads, each taking a turn in front then drifting back into the vacuum created by their team mates.

I used the bonnet of a shiny new Mercedes to write notes, much to the displeasure of its large German owner who gestured me away angrily. As I moved on, ANC flew past and a *bidon* half full of water, jettisoned for maximum lightness in the surge for the line, soared through the air to make a satisfying dent in the side of my friend's car.

Without the low-profile bikes and space-age helmets that characterised the top Continental teams, and with little expertise in this type of event, the Britons did well to finish 19th out of 23 teams. It was noticeable that Paul Watson had found the pace too much and was dropped, along with Steve Swart, before the finish.

No one was pleased with the prospect of the transfer from Berlin to Stuttgart next day. The riders had just begun to find their road legs and were faced with a flight down through East Germany to the West and Stuttgart, arriving in a thunderstorm. For the personnel it was even worse, with a horrendous 500-mile drive with the team vehicles through the Corridor, past the speed traps, the ancient Skodas, Ladas and Wartburgs of East Germany and across the border.

Officially, the Tour de France did not exist for East Germany, but we did find at least one closet cycling fan. As we waited at the border to pay out 5 Deutschmarks for a visa, the East German guard, after a few furtive glances to make sure that his colleagues couldn't hear, asked for a cycling cap as a souvenir, although he refused to waive the visa fee in return.

Shergold, Taylor and I arrived at 8 pm that night on our last drop of petrol (we had been unable to find the official Tour fuelling point and Capper had failed to supply his mechanics with any money for the journey), to land in the middle of a team talk between Woutters and his team manager. The subject was Watson, who rather than go out to train in the rain had stayed in his hotel room to use the static rollers.

'I don't know what's wrong with Paul,' said Capper in exasperation. 'The rest of the lads were prepared to go out in the rain. He's out of form, irritable and even he doesn't know why. Tomorrow I think Guy should go for the mountain prizes . . . he's the man in form on short climbs.'

'No, no,' replied Woutters, 'Gallopin is no climber. We must go for the catch sprints, win some cash. Get Elliott up to the front.'

And so the argument raged until it was eventually decided that the next day's two stages, from Karlsrühe to Stuttgart and from Stuttgart to Pforzheim, would be played by ear.

One man, at least, was looking happier. Palov the Czech defector was away from the East. For the first time he could allow himself a smile.

Prologue: West Berlin individual time trial, 6.1 kilometres, 51.452 kilometres an hour

Thursday, July 1

A suffocating blanket of humidity greeted the 207 riders for the Tour Prologue, a flat 4 miles up and down the Kurfürstendamm in Berlin's inner city. All feared that the oppressive heat might follow the Tour all the way to Paris – except of course the Colombians. Prologue specialist Jelle Nijdam of the Dutch Super Confex team (managed by former world champion Jan Raas) took the race's first yellow jersey by 3 seconds, beating off a strong challenge from Lech Piasecki of Poland and Stephen Roche.

Roche confirmed his status as one of the Tour favourites, although the Irishman was far from overjoyed with the title.

'I was hoping to hide early on and stay away from the pressure, but that will be difficult now,' he said on the way back to his Carrera team car.

The other fancied Tour riders took a more relaxed approach, with Sean Kelly, two-time winner Laurent Fignon and America's Andy Hampsten riding well within themselves and preferring to conserve their energies for the tougher challenges ahead.

Best of the ANC-Halfords team was Malcolm Elliott, celebrating his 26th birthday with a time of 7 minutes, 31.6 seconds – 25 seconds behind the winner.

1, Jelle Nijdam (NL) Super Confex, 7 mins, 06.80 secs.
2, Lech Piasecki (POL) Del Tongo, 3 secs behind.
3, Stephen Roche (IRE) Carrera, at 7 secs.
4, Guido Bontempi (ITAL) Carrera, same time.
5, Milan Jurco (CZE) Supermercati, at 8 secs.
6, Didi Thurau (WG) Roland-Skala, same time.
44, Malcolm Elliott (GB) ANC, at 25 secs.
57, Adrian Timmis (GB) ANC, at 27 secs.
109, Steven Swart (NZ) ANC, at 38 secs.

129, Guy Gallopin (FRA) ANC, at 41 secs.

143, Paul Watson (GB) ANC, at 44 secs.

161, Kvetoslav Palov (CZE) ANC, at 48 secs.

168, Bernard Chesneau (FRA) ANC, at 50 secs.

172, Graham Jones (GB) ANC, at 51 secs.

202, Shane Sutton (AUS) ANC, at 1 min, 05 secs.

Yellow jersey: Jelle Nijdam.

Stage 1: Berlin, 105.5 kilometres, 48.118 kilometres an hour

Friday, July 2

The site of Adolf Hitler's former headquarters, the Reichstag, by the Berlin Wall was the incongruous venue for the first stage proper of the Tour de France. Watched by the impassive border guards, the teams set off one by one to the Brandenburg Gate, the official starting point, before wheeling away at a fearsome pace over the undulating 67 miles through the suburbs of the divided city. The morning again belonged to Raas and his well-drilled Super Confex team, with 25-year-old Dutchman Nico Verhoeven getting away in a break of five riders to win the finishing sprint by a wheel length from Italy's Giovanni Bottoia. The stage also saw the first casualty of the Tour when, after 50 miles, 32 riders went down in a fall, among them ANC's Kvetoslav Palov and Steve Swart. The Czech and the New Zealander escaped injury; not so fortunate was Stefano Giuliani of the Supermercati team. While his countryman Bottoia was fighting it out with Verhoeven along Martin Luther King Strasse, Giuliani was on his way to hospital with a broken collarbone.

1, Nico Verhoeven (NL) Super Confex, 2 hours, 11 mins, 33 secs.

2, Giovanni Bottoia (BEL) Supermercati, same time.

3, Patrick Vershueren (BEL) Roland-Skala, same time.

4, Pascal Simon (FRA) Z-Peugeot, same time.

5, Theo De Rooy (NL) Panasonic, same time.

6, Lech Piasecki (POL) Del Tongo, same time.

17, Malcolm Elliott, 23 secs behind.

32, Guy Gallopin, same time.

57, Steven Swart, same time.

60, Graham Jones, same time.

67, Kvetoslav Palov, same time.

76, Bernard Chesneau, same time.

132, Shane Sutton, same time.

148, Adrian Timmis, same time.

199, Paul Watson, same time.

Yellow jersey: Lech Piasecki.

Stage 2: West Berlin team time trial, 40.5 kilometres, 54.200 kilometres an hour

Friday, July 2

Roche's Carrera team produced a disciplined display to take the afternoon's team time trial, which ran a circular 26 miles along the Wall to finish again at Martin Luther King Strasse. ANC- Halfords were over 2½ minutes adrift and their lack of practice in this sort of organised team effort showed. 'It was hard,' said Elliott later, 'but we improved as it went on.' It may have helped if the team's specialised time trial bikes with lightweight frames and 'cow horn' handlebars had arrived, but team manager Capper had experienced some difficulty in getting supplies, and the team had to go on their road bikes dressed up with a rear disc wheel. Poland's Lech Piasecki, who had finished sixth in the morning's Stage 1, retained his yellow jersey thanks to the second placing of his Del Tongo team.

1, Carrera, 44 mins, 50 secs.

2, Del Tongo, 8 secs behind.

3, Panasonic, at 27 secs.

4, Toshiba-Look, at 36 secs.

5, Système U, at 37 secs.

6, Z-Peugeot, at 1 min.

19, ANC-Halfords at 2 mins, 33 secs.

Yellow jersey: Lech Piasecki.

CHAPTER 3

THE OPEN ROAD

OF THE 2,629 MILES AND 25 stages of the 1987 Tour de France, eventual winner Stephen Roche probably walked less than 800 yards. Cyclists don't like travelling on two feet when they are racing and the team management will go to any lengths to help them avoid it. So when they are not actually on their bikes, Tour riders are in the back of team cars being transported to the start of a stage and after a stage they are met again and whisked away to their overnight stop, where they shower, get massage, eat and rest – in that order. They don't like hotels without lifts.

As Tour debutants in a foreign land, and without a potential winner to wrap in cotton wool, the nine riders of ANC had to do a bit more walking than someone like Roche or Sean Kelly.

But, with the exception of two notable occasions after mountain stages later on, there were no real complaints. Indeed, many of the British team hadn't mastered the art of getting off their feet as often as possible. Palov, in particular, drove Capper to distraction.

'Look at him,' the team manager would grumble as Omar mooned past on yet another unnecessary mission. 'Why can't he learn to get on his back in his room and rest? Kelly will be on his bed with his feet up the wall by now.'

With stages beginning at around 11 am, most teams would breakfast lightly at 7.30, return to bed for an hour and then tuck in to a large meal. All cyclists have their fads and fancies but a healthy diet with plenty of fruit and vegetables is considered as important for a professional as training. A good stomach and proficient digestion plus the ability to retain the vital nutrients are vital. On a long, strenuous stage, a rider may lose as much as eight pounds in body weight.

A typical day's eating for a Tour de France competitor during the actual race would consist of . . .

> **Breakfast**. Usually traditional to the rider's country but often bread rolls with jam, honey or cheese. Muesli is almost universally part of the breakfast ritual. A few riders will drink coffee but most prefer non-gaseous mineral water or tea.
>
> **Pre-race meal** (2–3 hours before the start). Pasta (usually spaghetti) with cheese, omelette, plain yoghurt (sometimes with sugar stirred in), tea or mineral water.
>
> **On the move**. A lot of the Continental teams like tea in the *bidons*, although almost as many will opt for a mixture of glucose and water or just plain water. Fruit cake, jam, honey, banana sandwiches. In desperate circumstances riders will try a Coke (for the caffeine) or glucose tablets to get through should they run out of fuel.
>
> **After the race**. Some riders will have a snack before the evening meal although a lot of *directeurs sportifs* believe you should not eat anything until dinner.
>
> **Dinner**. Salad starters. Fish or steak course with fresh vegetables, usually with pasta or rice. Sweet is usually a pudding (never ice cream) along with fresh apples or other fruit, yoghurt and the cheese board.

After the pre-race meal, the riders would climb into the team Peugeots and be transported down to the start. Most stage starts on major Tours are in town squares or main streets. While the inner area of riders and team cars is strictly cordoned and policed, the local populace can watch their heroes as they circle around on their bikes, spread themselves across the bonnets of their team vehicles and sign in at registration, where the major stars are announced in great style over the loudspeakers. While figures like Roche and two-time Tour winner Laurent Fignon lapped up all the adulation, posing on the podium, waving to the crowd, most of the ANC riders, unused to and embarrassed by all the attention, would try and get on and off the platform as quickly as possible . . . preferably hidden inside a large group of other riders.

I quickly got into the routine. Drive down with the riders, a delicious black coffee served by the equally delicious and equally dark girl in the Café de Colombia caravan, then a quick tour of the square and the English-speaking riders to see if there were any interesting quotes. Then, when the warning whistle went to prepare for the off, climb back into one of the cars and steam off after the race.

While the riders warmed up at moderate pace through the neutralised zone – the few miles out of town to the official starting place where the same honoured and beaming gendarme stood every day – the Tour cavalcade would sort itself out into its strictly controlled order.

One hour ahead was the publicity caravan, the circus-like parade of strangely decorated vehicles whose sponsorship takes care of most of the Tour budget. These include an incredible array of weird craft advertising anything from beer to condoms. While sporting purists may turn their noses up at the blatant commercialism, the publicity caravan with its stunts – one of the Michelin men had learned to ride complete stages standing on his motorbike – music and free gifts did keep the patient cycling fans lining the roadsides in their thousands entertained until the police outriders and the whistles and car horns of the first official vehicles heralded the appearance of the leaders and the spectators' brief few seconds' sight of the Tour as it flashed by in a dazzle of colour and chrome.

Behind the *peloton* (the main pack of riders) drove the race director, followed by the number one team cars containing the *directeur sportif* and one mechanic, sticking as far as possible to the right-hand lane and in an order governed by the placing of a team's leading rider.

After the first days in Berlin ANC were invariably in the 20s, so even Woutters in the lead car had his view of the race limited to a few distant flashes of wheels and saddles. And while I had a ringside seat of the personal daily struggles of ANC, the machinations of the race for the yellow jersey and even stages remained confined to the occasional brief announcements from Radio Tour, the short-wave race broadcast coming from the director's vehicle.

Radio Tour would transmit news of any breakaways and endeavour to keep *directeurs sportifs* abreast of developments in the bunch, including any rider who had punctured or needed food or water.

In the left lane were the cars of the journalists and the motorbikes carrying the TV cameramen and newspaper photographers ('the bravest men in the race' according to Phil Liggett of Channel 4), while zipping in and out on a sort of freelance basis were the open-topped Peugeot 205s of Vitascorbol, the Tour's paramedics. Their undoubted star was a magnificent raven-haired lady on a huge Kawasaki.

Finally, perhaps 2 miles distant from the actual leaders, were the back-up cars, which would go up to the front when the *directeur sportif* ahead decided to stop for a pee and whose other main task was to support any team riders dropped off the back of the bunch. When they couldn't offer support there were still the yellow-painted Mavic Peugeots, the neutral service vehicles who would do a wheel change or adjust gears or saddles for any rider. In all, the whole vast colourful convoy constituted a moving city of 3,000 people – flowing, accelerating, slowing and accelerating again across the closed roads of France like a huge, ever-changing amoeba.

At the start of every stage the ANC team would split up for the day – the riders onto their bikes to do battle, a mechanic in each team car, one with Woutters in front and one with Capper in the back-up. Fraser, the head *soigneur*, would take Friedhelm, his German subordinate, and head off to the halfway feeding point (*ravitaillement*), while Sabino, the youngest *soigneur*, in the ANC Citroën turbo estate would escort one of the other mechanics in the Iveco van to that night's overnight destination close to the stage end.

Of the drivers involved, Woutters and Griffiths, when he arrived, were the most experienced, Capper the flashiest, Angus the safest and Sabino possibly the worst, not just in the team but the whole of France.

A team car driver needs the skill and concentration of a rally driver, not only to follow the race at desperate speed through the narrow streets of rural towns and down precipitous mountain sides in the Alps and Pyrenees but also to keep an eye on the rear mirror. There he may spot a rider who has punctured or gone through a bad patch and is coming back through the convoy to rejoin the *peloton*. Accidents are inevitable and happen at the rate of one a day on Tour, but the rider always comes first. Any driver opening the door on the left-hand, wrong, side is fined by the *commissaires*.

Hardly surprisingly, after a week of this most cars have scrapes or bumps and smoking, strained gear boxes.

Nevertheless, when the Tour ends and Peugeot, the suppliers, put the official cars up for auction they are snapped up by enthusiasts in the same sort of spirit that characterises the fans at the roadside, who will take home and treasure the cheap hand-outs and free gifts – even bags of rubbish jettisoned from the Tour caravan – although some of the pretty girls lining the road blanched or blushed, according to their natures, at the free condoms.

Stage 3 of the Tour ran a hilly, humid 145 miles from Karlsrühe to Stuttgart in south-west Germany. Ward, who invariably played things strictly by the book, had applied for and obtained permission for me to ride alongside him in the lead car, a singular honour for a journalist, although, as I was quickly to discover, not the ideal way to follow the sharp end of the race.

To the sound of blaring car horns, a brass band and church bells, and with a helicopter chopping overhead, we motored out of Karlsrühe at 40 miles an hour in pursuit of the pack who had got stuck in at high speed to the day's work.

Five hours following a stage of the Tour de France soon leaves you immune to surprise. Like when the car you're travelling in squeals downhill at 60 miles per hour through the narrow crowded streets of a town and a rider overtakes going even faster. Or when a steep hill slows the convoy down to 20 miles per hour and a group of riders go past in pursuit of the pack. The whole frantic experience is like one of the rides in Disney World, a slow crank to the top, a breathless downhill plunge and some high-speed cruising when the land levels out.

While each stage is a race in itself, there are also, to keep the millions entertained en route and to ensure the riders don't spend the day sightseeing, cash prizes for intermediate sprints (sponsored by Catch, a French insecticide manufacturer) and climbs (sponsored by Café de Colombia), the sprints usually centred on a village or town and the climbs at the summit of a hill or col.

After 14 miles the signs appeared at the roadside counting down the riders to the first Catch sprint and Ward strained his ears in the hope of hearing an ANC name on Radio Tour.

'*Premier, Bontempi, suivi par Kelly et Duclos-Lasalle,*' announced Radio Tour dispassionately. Ward sighed in disappointment.

'Our riders are all afraid to try, they fear they will use all their energy and not reach Paris,' said the *directeur sportif.*

Four miles later, on the third-category climb to the Cote de Volkersbach (climbs are graded according to severity), came trouble. Sutton and Chesneau, pulverised by the unaccustomed and punishing pace at the front, had been dropped and were coming slowly back towards us as the other team cars went round them. As we pulled alongside, the Frenchman's sweating, suffering face turned towards his *directeur sportif* in helpless entreaty.

'Finished,' said Woutters with some finality, and motored on to leave the struggling duo to the mercies of Capper and Fisher in the second car.

Chesneau and Sutton were not quite ready to capitulate, however. Working with a rider from the Kas team in a desperate alliance, each taking a brief turn in front, they repassed us within a few miles.

'*Bidon,*' croaked Ches in between a fit of coughing as he pulled alongside. Ward whipped the plastic water bottle out of the window and handed it to the rider but exploded when he was handed a full one back.

'You see,' grumbled Woutters, 'his mind . . . not right.'

Nor was the Belgian overjoyed when Paul Watson dropped back to ferry some bottles from the car to his team mates, stuffing the larger plastic water bottles into the rear pockets of his jersey.

'That's not his job, he is not a *domestique.* His job is to ride; the *domestiques* must come back for the water.'

But even I could see that the *domestiques* were having their work cut out to stay in the race, never mind fulfil their appointed duties.

Most experienced mechanics – the ones who have been on major Tours before – are grateful to snatch some lost sleep during a stage. Steve Snowling was adept at this, knowing he would be woken if needed, but Steve Taylor in Woutters' car was wide awake and eagerly taking in his first exposure to a major Continental stage race.

After 80 miles he was called into action for the first time when the radio, amid news of the race ahead, requested: '*Voiture ANC au peloton.*' Ward accelerated out of line and, with his horn sounding, motored up through the convoy while all the other service cars, obeying a sort of rough and ready Tour Highway Code, did their best to get out of the way.

There in front was Adrian Timmis signalling that he had punctured. This was Taylor's chance to impress Ward and he didn't fail. As Timmis pulled into the side, and Woutters came to a full stop, Taylor, clutching a wheel, was out of the car and running. While Timmis stood over the bike holding up one end, Taylor changed, picked up the flatted wheel and pushed Timmis off again, running all the time with the old wheel.

It didn't take much imagination to work out what could happen if a wheel was left on the road for a few seconds and a rider appeared from behind. It was an impressive operation in forward motion and I timed it at just over 21 seconds.

While Taylor climbed out of the sunroof to attach the wheel to the roof clamps, Ward was watching Watson, who had hung back, pace Timmis back to the pack.

By now I knew what was coming and, sure enough: 'That is not up to him. That is not his job, Watson is not a *domestique,*' said our unforgiving *directeur sportif*. Poor Paul, it seemed, could do nothing right.

By now we had lost Shane and Chesneau again and with 30 miles to go Graham Jones appeared in front, dropped from the main pack as the attacks began in front.

'Give us a *bidon,*' said Jones to Taylor as we pulled up to him. The mechanic handed him a water bottle out of the window but obviously didn't know the tricks of the trade. As we motored on Jones was left screaming in frustration: 'Pull! Pull!'

'What's he on about?' asked Taylor.

'He needs a pull; here, I'll show you,' said Woutters, slowing down until Graham came alongside again.

'*Bidon*,' said Ward, handing one out of the window, then immediately accelerating as Jones clasped it firmly. The rider shot forward like a skier on a tow.

'You see,' said Ward, 'only 2 metres but it gives his legs a rest. Now he has impetus.'

So that was how it was done. Taylor was flabbergasted. He'd been a good-class racing cyclist in Britain for a long time but he'd never seen this sort of sophisticated aid-giving. Nor had the other mechanic, Shergold, another former racer. Palov the Czech, who had only just turned professional, didn't know the trick either, and while Capper throughout the Tour tried to get him to take a push, Omar stubbornly and consistently refused.

Strangely, Ward wasn't averse to risking the wrath of the *commissaires* by pushing a struggling rider but drew the line elsewhere. In the last 20 miles of a stage, when the real racing begins and the danger of cars weaving in and out of the bunch is obvious, no feeding is allowed. So when Swart dropped back to ask Ward for water the Belgian was obdurate.

'No, no, it is not permitted now,' he told the red-faced New Zealander.

'Oh, come on, everybody else is!' stormed Swart.

Grudgingly, Woutters handed out a *bidon*: 'But you see, we will be fined for this and you will be penalised some time,' he warned.

The last 14 miles into Stuttgart were characterised by a series of short sharp climbs and these proved too much for Watson and Gallopin, who both dropped off the back. On the Tour's first proper road stage, five ANC riders had been left by the pack, one of them for good.

Poor Chesneau had finished almost half an hour behind the

stage winner, Acacio da Silva of Portugal, and Ward had worked out long before the finishing line that Ches would be outside the time limit.

Chesneau was inconsolable. He was out of his country's national Tour, the dream of every French schoolboy, and the race hadn't even reached French soil. That night he departed by train to Paris, looking like a spaniel who had had his bone taken away.

We had travelled over 140 miles in a shade under 5½ hours and at an average speed of 25 miles an hour. While the taut and sweat-streaked faces and blank eyes told what the day had taken out of the riders, I couldn't help noticing how much it had taken out of Ward Woutters, too. Paris was still over 2,000 miles away.

Surely, but not so slowly, the race was heading for French soil, with most riders anxious to get Germany behind and return to the Tour's traditional roots. Stage 4 would take us from Stuttgart to Pforzheim in the morning of July 5, with lunch in the gold town of Pforzheim, and another stage into Strasbourg and France in the afternoon. ANC had had the harshest of baptisms, with most complaining of the fierce initial pace and the humid conditions as well as aching muscles. Sutton, Watson, Jones and Gallopin were clearly struggling.

Even Stephen Roche had remarked in Stuttgart's Schloss Platz before Stage 4: 'If the race continues at this sort of pace we'll arrive on the Champs-Elysées in coffins.'

It seemed a brutal way to make a living.

Stage 3: Karlsrühe to Stuttgart, 219 kilometres, 40.112 kilometres an hour

Saturday, July 4

After the disruptive transfer from Berlin to Stuttgart (by plane for the riders and a 500-mile drive through the Corridor and through the Wall for the team personnel) the Tour had to start again. Many riders did not have the time or inclination to train on arriving in Stuttgart accompanied by a thunderstorm and there was active resentment as they lined up for Stage 3, which took them 145 miles from Karlsrühe through the immaculate villages and picturesque countryside of Baden-Württemberg back to Stuttgart and its hilly finish. Even the genial Roche was finding it hard to keep smiling, admitting feeling 'uptight' and saying: 'It mucks up the whole system.' Some of the resentment must have spilled over into a stage highlighted by early attacks and ferocious chases. With 30 miles left, a break of 22 riders developed including the little Frenchman Charly Mottet, one of a dozen men considered likely eventual winners. A late charge by Portugal's sole Tour representative Acacio da Silva gave him a comfortable win from Carrera's Swiss *domestique* Erich Maechler, although Maechler could not complain as new wearer of the yellow jersey, a position he was to hold for almost a week.

While the Tour is almost sacred in its native France, it was obviously considered less so in Germany and finish line officials were puzzled to count an extra rider as the bunch came through . . . a young West German complete with official number had infiltrated the bunch and rode over the line with them. The intruder won his headlines but his ultimate fate remained uncertain as he was carted off by the Stuttgart Polizei.

1, Acacio da Silva (POR) Kas, 5 hours, 27 mins, 35 secs.
2, Erich Maechler (SWI) Carrera, 2 secs behind.
3, Jorg Müller (SWI) PDM, at 9 secs.

4, Dag-Otto Lauritzen (NOR) 7-Eleven, at 14 secs.

5, Jean-Claude LeClercq (FRA) Toshiba-Look, at 48 secs.

6, Féderico Echave (SPA) BH, same time.

76, Adrian Timmis, 5 mins, 55 secs behind.

79, Malcolm Elliott, same time.

113, Kvetoslav Palov, same time.

174, Steve Swart, at 8 mins, 13 secs.

190, Guy Gallopin, at 14 mins, 21 secs.

191, Paul Watson, at 17 mins, 39 secs.

197, Shane Sutton, at 25 mins, 17 secs.

201, Graham Jones, at 27 mins, 24 secs.

203, Bernard Chesneau, at 29 mins, 23 secs.

Yellow jersey: Erich Maechler.

Stage 4: Stuttgart to Pforzheim, 79 kilometres, 43.333 kilometres an hour

Sunday, July 5

Belgians Herman Frison and Marc Sergeant turned July 5 into a great double for their country with lone wins on the split stage day which saw the race finally out of Germany and back on home ground at Strasbourg. Before the start of the short 52 miles from Stuttgart to Pforzheim, many riders had complained about the unaccustomedly fast pace up front and the morning was made for a breakaway. Frison attacked almost as soon as the race climbed out of Stuttgart and, with the bunch taking a more leisurely approach to the day's proceedings, he quickly had a 3-minute lead. With 16 miles left the Belgian had upped his lead to over 4 minutes, until almost reluctantly the bunch took up the chase. Frison, however, was out of sight, picking up the stage's one intermediate sprint and its cash prize for his Roland-Skala team as well as the two climbing awards. Tiring visibly towards the end after his solo heroics Frison still stayed almost 1½ minutes ahead of the bunch, where the massed sprint was taken by Jean-Paul Van Poppel of Super Confex.

1, Herman Frison (BEL) Roland-Skala, 1 hour, 49 mins, 23 secs.

2, Jean-Paul Van Poppel (NL) Super Confex, 1 min, 28 secs behind.

3, Stefano Allocchio (ITAL) Supermercati, same time.

4, Phil Anderson (AUS) Panasonic, same time.

5, Davis Phinney (US) 7-Eleven, same time.

6, Johan Capiot (BEL) Roland-Skala, same time.

25, Guy Gallopin, same time.

67, Kvetoslav Palov, same time.

103, Graham Jones, same time.

144, Adrian Timmis, same time.

165, Malcolm Elliott, same time.

175, Steve Swart, same time.

200, Paul Watson, same time.

202, Shane Sutton, at 2 mins, 19 secs.

Yellow jersey: Erich Maechler.

Stage 5: Pforzheim to Strasbourg, 112.5 kilometres, 44.267 kilometres an hour

Sunday, July 5

Lunch was taken at the gold-producing town of Pforzheim where, as well as an interminable speech by the 83-year-old race director Jacques Goddet and an equally lengthy reply by the town's mayor, journalists were also presented with gold-bar key rings – imitation unfortunately.

Not to be outdone by Frison, his Belgian countryman Sergeant of the Joker team, prompted by his *directeur sportif*, decided he would try his luck in the afternoon's 75 miles into France. Stage 5 was characterised by the first serious climbing on the third-category Cote de Dennach, where we caught our first sight of Colombia's 'winged angel' Luis Herrera at the front of the bunch. But when the contour lines flattened again almost halfway through the stage, Sergeant made his decisive attack and, helped by a following wind, managed to build up a lead of 4 minutes. Sergeant was first across the Rhine and onto French soil at 60 miles. Customs formalities had been relaxed for the day!

Shortly afterwards the green and white jerseys of Super Confex appeared at the front of the bunch, trying to set up a win for their master sprinter Van Poppel, and the chase was on. With only 6 miles left, Sergeant's lead was down to 1½ minutes and the Belgian was beginning to look fallible, but rocking and weaving into the 2,000-year-old city of Strasbourg he managed to hold on for a famous double. Thirteen seconds behind Sergeant the bunch came charging down the main street, with Sean Kelly showing a first flash of form to finish third behind Bruno Wojtinek of France. 'At the line some imbecile told me I had won,' said Wojtinek, 'and it took some time to sink in that I'd only come second. This morning's sprint [into Pforzheim] was very dangerous but I felt better this afternoon on a much wider road. I felt more at ease.'

Less happy was Stephen Roche, who felt that Carrera had preferred to try to save Maechler's yellow jersey than look after their team leader. 'I was left completely on my own,' said Roche.

ANC-Halfords won their first tangible reward of the Tour when Graham Jones picked up a huge bunch of flowers and £100 for the Prix de l'Amabilité – the Mr Nice Guy award – to go with Omar Palov's £30 for second place in an intermediate sprint.

1, Marc Sergeant (BEL) Joker, 2 hours, 32 mins, 29 secs.
2, Bruno Wojtinek (FRA) Z-Peugeot, 13 secs behind.
3, Sean Kelly (IRE) Kas, same time.
4, Davis Phinney (US) 7-Eleven, same time.

5, Roberto Amadio (ITAL) Supermercati, same time.

6, Martial Gayant (FRA) Système U, same time.

79, Adrian Timmis, same time.

118, Malcolm Elliott, same time.

162, Kvetoslav Palov, same time.

171, Shane Sutton, same time.

191, Steve Swart, at 2 mins, 14 secs.

198, Graham Jones, at 4 mins, 14 secs.

200, Guy Gallopin, at 12 mins, 25 secs.

202, Paul Watson, same time.

Yellow jersey: Erich Maechler.

CHAPTER 4

FOUL PLAY

WHILE THE TOUR WAS MAKING its big loop of France, Pat Cash the Australian tennis player was earning £100,000 for his winning Wimbledon fortnight and golfer Nick Faldo, already a millionaire, was adding £70,000 to his healthy bank balance by taking the British Open Championship in four days. Rich pickings indeed for so little comparative time and effort, and small wonder that cyclists consider themselves the paupers of professional sport. For his month-long, back-breaking and debilitating agonies in midsummer France, Roche won £41,000 from the Tour (annual profit 17 million francs a year), a sum which included a bizarrely unattractive holiday flat in the Pyrenees and a Peugeot 403 saloon – not forgetting a Peugeot 205 Junior, £1,800 and a silver map of France for his stage win at Poitiers. The yellow jersey of race victor and subsequent increased marketing value earned him a contract for 1988 of £400,000 a year from his new team Fagor, but for that he would be expected to spend ten months in the saddle, deny himself most of the rights and pleasures of the average man and live out of a suitcase in a season of almost non-stop travel. Fatigue would erode his body and mind and he would risk life and limb on lonely mountain passes and their crazed, hair-raising descents.

If the Tour de France is about mind-numbing courage, it is also a monument to greed, ambition and crass commercialism, which spawn in their turn dubious ethics and questionable tactics. It's a contest that's designed not for the competitor but for the acquisitive commodity brokers who hawk it around Europe to produce the highest available profit.

That is why the 1987 Tour de France spent its first four days in Germany and why, as well as the charter out of Berlin and back to the West, it also contained two long transfers by train between stage towns that had outbid others for the honour of playing host to the Tour.

Coca-Cola had outbid Perrier before the 1987 Tour with £1 million, which bought the rights to be official drinks supplier, and Crédit Lyonnais, the French bank, paid a small fortune to have its name on the yellow jersey of race leader (although camera firm Ricoh had the rights to the riders' backs).

In the year before the 1987 Tour its foundations had been rocked by a row over sponsorship with co-director Félix Lévitan, who was sacked by its owners, the Amaury family who also run the French sports paper *L'Équipe*. Lévitan's replacement, an out-and-out hard-nosed businessman with no interest in sport called François Naquet-Radiguet, had indicated that, despite the Tour's huge profits, fees would go up in 1988.

The riders may be the spectacle, but in this commercial power play they are really the bit players required to perform their heroics to the tune of ringing cash tills.

It doesn't take long in witnessing a Tour at first hand to realise that physically and mentally the human body wasn't designed for something so eroding. At least the organisers recognise this by turning a blind eye (or at the most handing out what amounts to token punishment) to team directors who offer their charges a little outside assistance and the riders who accept it.

Doping is a banned topic in cycling conversations and any journalist covering the Tour automatically becomes a part of the same conspiracy, but the rumours and nudges and winks, the miming of a needle in the arm after some particularly bravura feat in the mountains or sprints, are hard to ignore. So are the physical signs of riders remaining jaunty, wide-eyed and full of life after seven hours of punishment in the saddle.

In the sixties, when cyclists, many from humble backgrounds, were tempted into drug indiscretions by the increase in prize money that the Tour's commercial success produced, stimulants were used freely. In 1966 the first five finishers in the World Championships refused a dope test, including the five-times Tour de France winner Jacques Anquetil. It was Anquetil himself who said: 'Everyone in cycling dopes themselves and those who claim they don't are liars.'

Anquetil was subsequently suspended from the sport but reinstated within months. That he should go on to become a national hero of France and a respected TV and newspaper commentator shows how seriously his 'crime' was taken not just by the sport's rulers but also by the general public and how the unacceptable was on its way to becoming the commonplace.

Anquetil was dying of stomach cancer as he worked on the 1987 Tour and died shortly after Roche collected the victor's laurel wreath in Paris. He was 53, fulfilling the average predicted life expectancy of a professional cyclist almost exactly.

The history of the Tour is littered with headlines of positive testings and includes many of the great names of the sport.

Dutchman Joop Zoetemelk, winner in 1980 and still competing at the age of 42, was twice penalised for steroid use and the greatest rider of all, Eddy Merckx, was disqualified from the 1969 Giro d'Italia after testing positive, although he later claimed successfully that a spectator had handed him a spiked drink on one of the stages. Merckx, however, was less fortunate in 1977 towards the end of his career when, along with former world champion and fellow Belgian Freddy Maertens, tests showed the positive use of stimulants. Perhaps the most bizarre incident came in the 1978 Tour de France, when race leader Michel Pollentier of Belgium and Frenchman Antoine Guttierez were caught attempting an elaborate fraud to avoid detection during a urine test. Both riders had a bag of 'clean' urine strapped on their chests kept warm by body heat to allay suspicion and a tube ran down their arms so that hopefully they could squeeze out the safe sample for the tester, who wasn't fooled. Ironically, one of the guilty men's fiercest critics was Zoetemelk, who declared: 'Pollentier has distorted the race' . . . one year after his own first offence.

But it took the death of an Englishman on a sun-whitened French mountainside to open the eyes of the world to the fact that, even with widespread testing, athletes were still prepared to dope themselves towards the yellow jersey or simply through a crisis.

Tommy Simpson was the first Briton to compete on equal terms with the top Continentals and a former world champion, but it was his ordeal on Mont Ventoux near Avignon, one of the Tour's most legend-laden stages, that was to etch his name into the history of the sport.

On a furnace-hot July day and watched by millions of TV viewers, Simpson, after weaving and wobbling for yard after yard up the Ventoux climb, collapsed and died. At the time his death was attributed to heat exhaustion and heart failure but an autopsy later revealed traces of amphetamine in his body. More drugs were found among the rider's personal possessions. 'Put me back on my bike,' Simpson said as he lay on the granite mountainside – last words that speak of not only awesome courage but also the classic symptoms of stimulant abuse, as the drug removes any warning signals of encroaching exhaustion the body may be trying to give to the mind.

* * *

Nowadays on the Tour the yellow jersey and the first three finishers on the day are tested along with a couple at random . . . which still leaves plenty of odds for the gambler. Some will still take a chance with amphetamines but the game has become more sophisticated, with masking drugs to cover the corticosteroids, used to kill pain, or the steroids to build muscle mass and increase tolerance to training. As one team manager told me: 'We're one step ahead of the testers all the time. And the drugs are so easy to get. You just go round Europe and ask in chemists. Most will say "no" but you'll always find one who will sell them eventually.' Pressed on the number of riders in the Tour using drugs, the same manager said: 'Ninety-five per cent,' although on reflection he may have left 5 per cent 'clean' to protect the good name of his own team.

Looking down the cast list of the 1987 Tour, the great Irish cyclist Sean Kelly had been tested positive in 1984 and two-time winner Laurent Fignon in 1987 just before the Tour began. Frenchman Bernard Thevenet, Tour victor in 1975 and 1977, once admitted that he had 'ruined his health' by using corticosteroids. He was now managing the RMO team. Jeannie Longo, who won the women's 1987 'Tour Féminin', tested positive in a subsequent race.

During the 1987 Tour, testers obtained positive readings on Guido Bontempi of Roche's Carrera team, Silvano Contini of the Italian Del Tongo team and Dietrich Thurau of Roland-Skala, the same Thurau who had pursued Graham Jones down the Kurfürstendamm and so impressed Ward Woutters. All protested their innocence and as first offenders were given one month's suspended ban, fined £500 and demoted to last on the relevant stages, as well as incurring a ten-minute time penalty. All were free to continue the Tour. Bontempi, one of the sport's great sprinters, had been tested after he won Stage 7 from Épinal to Troyes and found to have traces of testosterone, the hormone. Quite naturally the Carrera team manager was amazed.

'What can I do, what can I say?' he asked. 'They found in the analysis a small amount of testosterone, the natural hormone secreted by the body. Guido swears by God that he has taken nothing. To show everyone the injustice of it all Guido has decided to stay on the Tour and to win another stage.'

In the French press, at least, the news that the winner of one of the major stages of the Tour was positive didn't cut much ice, being relegated in the sports newspaper *L'Équipe* to seven or eight paragraphs down page, surely an indictment in itself. Cycling *positifs* are plainly as newsworthy these days as minor soccer transfers.

'*Les Anglais sont terminés*,' yelled a teenage cycling fan clad in the gear of the French team Z-Peugeot. Our young friend was almost hugging himself with delight and offered reinforcement to the impression, given following our landing on French soil at Strasbourg, that not all the French were delighted by the prospect of an English team competing in their beloved Tour. Some of the roadside gestures and comments were graphic to say the least.

At Strasbourg, Ward Woutters and Roger the *soigneur* had departed 'for business reasons' and Phil Griffiths had arrived from Britain to take over as *directeur sportif*. Immediately, Capper had seized his chance and taken over in the lead Peugeot, leaving Griffiths the mopping-up operation in the second car.

The 112-mile stage from Strasbourg to Épinal through the Vosges mountains contained the first real climbing challenge on the Col du Champ du Feu after 40 miles. Literally translated it means Field of Fire and never was a hill more aptly named . . . for ANC-Halfords at least.

Our French friend hadn't been far wrong in his scornful verdict. As Griffiths topped the first rise on the first-category climb to the col he could see two orange saddles moving up through the forest in a sort of slow death march, while Radio Tour crackled the news that two other ANC riders had just been dropped by the main bunch twenty minutes ahead. It looked like being a long, hard day.

Griffiths was horror struck. Here he was on his first day as team director and he faced losing half his complement with the Tour not yet a week old.

'Christ, look at Graham, he's legless,' he said, as we pulled alongside Jones and Paul Watson.

Jones, his face grey with effort, kept his eyes glued firmly to the two feet of melting tarmac in front of his wheel while the sweat dripped steadily down his long nose. Watson, in contrast, looked positively chirpy, pedalling smoothly in a big gear and quite prepared to pass the time of day.

'What's happening up front?' he asked.

'Never mind that,' snapped Griffiths in his staccato manner. 'You've got two choices now, Paul. You can either make an effort and ride strongly to the finish and maybe get blown out or you can stay back here and get eliminated. Graham's gone, you've still got it, so either way tomorrow doesn't exist. Now drop down a gear and ride away from Graham – don't wait for him at all. I want you apart on this climb – the *commissaires* can't watch both of you.'

Watson nodded his agreement and within seconds had put 300 yards between himself and Jones.

'Right, Graham, bottle,' said Griffiths, handing a *bidon* out of the left-hand window. Jones clasped the bottle and Griffiths accelerated smoothly, dragging the rider uphill with the car.

As if by magic a *commissaire* on a motor cycle appeared, wagging his finger from side to side in rebuke. But the warning came with a resigned and sympathetic smile – he too could see that the end wasn't far away for Graham.

Griffiths was now in a dilemma. Capper in the lead car was up behind the bunch looking after the interests of Elliott, Timmis, Swart and Palov, while Sutton and Gallopin had been dropped and were going to need all the help going if they were to reach Épinal and stay in the Tour.

Jones was past all help and after 60 miles of painful effort finally came to Griffiths' aid.

'It's no good,' said Graham.

'Right, are you going to get off?' asked Griffiths immediately.

Jones nodded disconsolately and Griffiths sped away in pursuit of Watson, leaving Jones to be picked up by the 'broom wagon', the van and trailer that followed the race to mop up the failures.

By now Watson was 30 minutes behind the main bunch and it was clear that it was going to take more than a few pushes to save his skin. Griffiths decided to motor on, resigned to the fact that he had lost half his English contingent and two of his acknowledged climbers on the race's first major climb. The scornful forecast of Woutters in Berlin had come uncannily true.

After 75 miles another orange saddle loomed into view – Gallopin the Frenchman involved in his own lonely battle to get inside the time limit at Épinal. Sutton had somehow made it back to the bunch and now Griffiths could concentrate all his energies on making sure ANC didn't lose another rider. By now the *commissaire* had departed, perhaps in search of more worthy game, and Griffiths was able to employ the bottle trick for 20 seconds at a time, and when the spectators thinned out on lonely stretches of road all pretence went literally out of the window with Gallopin hanging on like grim death to the car door while Griffiths motored along at 60 miles per hour. A casual watcher would have been amazed by the extraordinary sight of a cyclist, one hand on the car and one hand on his handlebars and his legs going round like a hamster on a treadwheel, stuck like glue to the speeding Peugeot.

Nearer Épinal the crowds thickened again and Griffiths had to employ more sophisticated tactics.

Brandishing a rider's cap, the universal currency of the Tour, he called over a police motor cyclist.

'*Vous allez juste avant?*' asked Griffiths hopefully, pointing ahead

71

to the straining Gallopin. Without a word the motor cyclist, one of the 62-strong Garde Republicaine who police the race every year, shoved the ANC cap inside his blue uniform and accelerated away to station himself 10 yards ahead of his countryman.

Gallopin clued in immediately and positioned himself behind his elite pacer until, with the rider just safe inside the limit close to the finish, Gallopin was allowed to ride the last few kilometres unaided.

Was it cheating? Perhaps, but Gallopin was a Frenchman in his national Tour and two days later the race was due to pass through his home village of Corbeil on the outskirts of Paris. He had to be admired for the guts that had kept him going for mile after lonely mile.

Griffiths was simply adopting the universal tactics of any team director with a rider in trouble. Most of the team, in fact, regarded the police rider trick as a stroke of genius.

Even the Tour jury tacitly accept the 'illegal' pushing and pacing, with paltry fines – little more than a slap on the wrist – handed out on a daily basis to the transgressors.

In the hotel that night, 20 miles outside the town of Épinal, the inquests began. Watson was bouncing around seemingly unaffected, while Jones, his cheeks and eyes sunken into his skull, drank a farewell beer. As always it was hard to think of something to say to a sportsman who had failed. Griffiths wanted Watson banned from cycling for 'walking out of the Tour'.

'Did he walk out really?' I asked.

'As good as,' replied Griffiths. 'There was nothing wrong with him. Graham Jones has had one Tour too many – he was in his lowest gear possible and still legless, while Watson was cruising, doing nothing. It's more a question of what Paul wants to do. It wasn't his legs, he's got the strength as you yourself could see. It's obviously worth looking into.'

Capper interjected: 'Chesneau and Graham Jones were legless,

Watson was headless. He was looking at the route profiles every night and saying: "How am I going to do this, Christ look at this climb, look at that climb!" Basically he just talked himself out of it.'

'What about the effect on team morale?' I asked.

'Basically we are here for survival,' said Griffiths. 'We have to come here for two or three years to achieve the things we want to achieve, but from a survival point of view it doesn't make a great deal of difference. The lads will get more help from the three *soigneurs* and three mechanics and various managers and hopefully we'll still get the rest of the guys through. The toughness of the climbs and the speed of the race has shown the weak people up straight away for whatever reason. They have now been processed, if you like.'

'Do you wish you could start again?' I asked Capper.

'Yes, I wish we could,' replied the team manager, 'and we'd have eight riders left now. I wouldn't have had Chesneau in a team of mine but we were dragged into it. I'd have kept the one Frenchman. You could see the difference between Guy and Paul today. Guy was carrying on even though he was suffering just as much as Paul . . . Guy KNEW what was going to happen.

'The trouble now is Paul has got to start from scratch again. Any reputation he had is gone now and he'll have to prove himself all over again.'

Watson, however, didn't seem too concerned about his reputation. Next day, as the other riders set off to drive back down to Épinal and Stage 7 to Troyes, he ordered Sabino, the little *soigneur*, to drive him the 100 kilometres to Paris in the Citroën estate.

Sabino was incensed but gave in eventually.

'Watson rang his *copine* in Paris first to tell her he was coming,' said the outraged Frenchman later. 'Watson . . . *petit con!*'

Nor was Paul Watson the only ANC rider to upset the much

maligned Sabino. Like all *soigneurs*, especially French ones, Sabino had his pride. The ANC job was his first with a cycling team but his brother was personal masseur to the great Sean Kelly in the Kas team and Sabino knew the score. He wasn't impressed with ANC-Halfords and their big boss.

'Their diet is not right, they don't get enough rest,' Sabino told me. 'ANC eat too much grease, too much fish, too much cream. And Kelly always he sits, rests, eats the right things. Sutton asked me to wash his jersey but I said: "*Non, non!*"' – Sabino raised his finger and wagged it from side to side – '"*Non, non*, even Sean Kelly does not ask that of his *soigneur.*"

'Sutton said to me: "Fucking, fucking this and that," but I still said "*Non*".

'OK, Kelly is a very big star and the telephone rings all the time for him. Sometimes he doesn't have time to wash his clothes so my brother does it for him. But Kelly never ask. Sutton . . . *petit con*, Capper . . . *grand con*, I do not wash jerseys for ANC.'

After the Massacre of the Field of Fire, ANC and the Tour travelled in three long days west from the Rhine Valley, below Paris and almost to the coast. They were stages made for the sprinters, the big men who specialise in the bunched charge for the line like Bontempi, his great Dutch rival Jean-Paul Van Poppel . . . and Malcolm Elliott.

Elliott, working without the organised tactical efforts offered by Carrera to Bontempi and Super Confex to Van Poppel, did well to finish 10th from Épinal into Troyes, although he was later elevated to ninth after Bontempi's indiscretion. Gallopin had produced a remarkable recovery, going off the front of the bunch at one point and earning ANC-Halfords some useful TV exposure, and Shane, too, seemed happier. At Troyes the Australian seemed almost drunk with emotion, missing his pal Watson and saying: 'Paul really went through it. He's a mate of mine and I've tried my best with him, telephoning him, advising him, but no good.'

Shane and Guy – the two married men – were now sharing rooms, which limited Shane's bantering chat.

'He now has to talk very slowly so I can understand,' said Gallopin with a smile.

At Troyes I climbed into the Peugeot brake behind Angus Fraser and his German subordinate Friedhelm to witness the *ravitaillement*, or halfway feed. In most long stages racers will swiftly run out of fuel and have to recharge at least once on the move.

Driving in the 23-strong convoy of identical vehicles we set off at high speed for the feeding point at 80 miles in the village of Bologne in the Haute-Marne.

Anyone in an official Tour team car is an instant celebrity but by now the novelty of being applauded as if we were riders by the roadside crowds was beginning to wear off, especially when at every set of lights French children, or sometimes their fathers, would stick their heads in through the window to demand a cycling cap. At other times we would be hailed by British cyclists following the Tour asking for a spare tube or a spare strap for their bikes. Angus would give them short shrift. During the drive, in between describing his asthma symptoms or the fights he had been in, Angus made it clear who was the boss *soigneur* in this particular team.

'Roger always wants tea in the *bidons*,' said the uncompromising Scot. 'That's what they do in Belgium. When Malcolm asked for tea in his *bidon* one day Roger said: "Ah, I told you so." But normally they just want water or Isostar . . . and that's what they get.'

I remarked to him that all the policemen lining the roadside at strategic points to keep the public off the road looked the same as the day before, and he looked at me scornfully.

'Of course they're the same, man. Look, this Tour is really four Tours in one. You've got the riders, the publicity caravan, the personnel and the police who travel ahead of the convoy all the time. They're the same bunch.'

* * *

75

At Bologne, Angus and Friedhelm squeezed themselves into ANC jerseys two sizes too small and along with the other team *soigneurs* settled down to wait, dangling the cloth '*musettes*' containing the riders' high-energy foods on their fingers. Just in front of us was one of the personnel from the American 7-Eleven outfit, a bleached and tanned blonde dressed in a ra-ra skirt like a cheerleader at a basketball game, an incongruous sight alongside the rest of the hoary-handed masseurs from all over Europe and South America who soothed away the riders' aches each night. I could envisage the problems of a rider thousands of miles and many days away from wife or sweetheart being slapped and pulled by an attractive female each night, or did they discipline themselves in that respect, too?

Finally the first police outrider heralded the leader, Frenchman Régis Clère determined to impress in his home region, on a lone breakaway, but ten seconds behind came the bunch in howling pursuit.

As if by magic, the six ANC riders infiltrated their way over to our side of the road and the *musettes* disappeared like a night mail train snatching its goods from a trackside stanchion. Without a pause in their fearsome rhythm and with both hands off the handlebars, they emptied the *musettes* swiftly into their rear jersey pockets and within seconds the race had disappeared up the road pursued by the roaring convoy of race directors and team cars, until all that was left to tell of their passing were a few scraps of paper wafting along the road in the slipstream and a posse of small boys racing each other to the discarded *musettes* at the end of the village.

Angus, Friedhelm and the rest of the *soigneurs* climbed back into the brakes and set off for the hectic dash to the finish.

Little Sabino, the third *soigneur*, spent his days in more leisurely fashion. Officially his job was to escort one of the mechanics in the slow, swaying Iveco containing the riders' suitcases and the thousands of pounds' worth of cycling spares to that night's stopover, but once inside the turbo Citroën Sabino found it hard to restrain himself, motoring off at high speed while the Iveco struggled on behind. It was a habit that was always getting him in hot water with Capper or Griffiths, who quite rightly didn't want the van breaking down somewhere in rural France leaving the riders without a change of clothes or the mechanics without the means to work on the bikes.

Sabino was a terrible driver, fidgeting, admiring himself in the mirror and serenading any passing female. His favourite trick behind a line of traffic at lights was to motor down the pavement asking each motorist in turn for directions until he reached the front where he would cut in. Nobody ever objected. As Capper had remarked, like the presidential limousine . . .

At the hotel, Sabino would join the queue of other *soigneurs* at reception for allocation of the rooms, ideally with one team together on one floor along with their masseurs, carry the suitcases into the right rooms and then relax to await the arrival of the team. He usually had a long wait. Without fail, the ANC team cars were always last back from the stage finish.

The words a *directeur sportif* learns to dread most are Radio Tour's '*chute dans le peloton*', which means someone has fallen, perhaps bringing down dozens of others, perhaps the yellow jersey, their team leader or race favourite. In the last 6 miles of the race's longest stage, the 175-mile 9th from Orléans to Renazé, there were four crashes on the narrow roads.

These triggered the massed charge of 23 lead cars towards the front, each trying to get as close to the accident as quickly as possible for the mechanics to dive out with handfuls of wheels in case one of their men had punctured or bent a rim.

The final crash allowed a break of five riders to get clear and there was instant panic in the *peloton* as they struggled and fought to disentangle themselves and set off in pursuit. Two riders threw punches at each other, while some of the others took off like cyclocross riders into the fields alongside in a bid to bypass the pile-up. After a week, the sight of gravel rash wounds, bruises and sticking plaster was becoming commonplace.

The paramedics of Vitascorbol were able to treat most minor injuries on the move, but a rider's first reaction after damaging himself is to carry on to the finish, burying whatever pain there is, and avoid being eliminated.

Most of the better-sponsored teams have their own doctor on Tour – ANC had Angus – and with a one in thirty chance of injury they were kept busy.

With their feet attached to toe clips, riders invariably land on their shoulders in a fall, and a broken collarbone is the most common fracture in the sport, just ahead of broken wrists and ribs. The wrists are invariably used in an effort to cushion a fall, and if a rider is first to go down there's a good chance of suffering rib injury when the others pile on top.

A professional cyclist's most inevitable source of complaint, however, is the perineum . . . the bum. I was soon to find out why.

Stage 6: Strasbourg to Épinal, 169 kilometres, 40.087 kilometres an hour

Monday, July 6

The main subject of debate in Strasbourg's Place Kleber, where the riders foregathered for the 112 miles to Épinal, was whether Carrera would try and defend Erich Maechler's yellow jersey or bow to Roche's wishes, let it go, and take some pressure off the team. In the end Carrera did keep it for Maechler – just. Cyrille Guimard, the wily and highly successful *directeur sportif* of France's Système U, and Christophe Lavainne, one of the team's *domestiques*, had worked out that, with Lavainne's consistent performances in the Tour to date, a win into Épinal by a minute or more would give the rider the yellow jersey – and his sponsors some valued publicity. After the ascents in the Vosges mountains a break of seven including Lavainne got away and, working together, gradually built a lead of close to 8 minutes. With 35 miles left Lavainne made his getaway with only Mexican Raúl Alcalá giving chase. By now the Carrera team had cottoned on that if Maechler was going to keep his yellow jersey they had better cut down Lavainne's lead to less damaging proportions and towed the bunch through the last 20 miles at top speed. Lavainne won easily and the countdown began – first Alcalá just over 1 minute behind, then the rest of the seven-man breakaway at 2 minutes 34 seconds, hotly pursued by the bunch, including a very hot and bothered Maechler who had held on to his yellow jersey by the skin of his teeth. Again Roche was an unhappy man at the finish. 'I wanted our team to wait for a while before starting to chase,' he said. 'I wanted to see if another team would chase instead. Then the others decided to get moving and there was nothing I could do.'

The warmth of the day and the speed of the racing produced some notable casualties including Gilbert Glaus of Switzerland, a former world amateur champion who ultimately joined ANC's Jones and Watson in the broom wagon. Another struggling rider was Dutch champion Adrie Van Der Poel of Pedro Delgado's PDM team. Van Der Poel, however, was to demonstrate the virtues of digging in and riding on to the finish . . . three days later he was to take the stage win from Orléans to Renazé.

1, Christophe Lavainne (FRA) Système U, 4 hours, 12 mins, 57 secs.

2, Raúl Alcalá (MEX), 7-Eleven, 1 min, 34 secs behind.

3, Manuel Jorge Domínguez (SPA) BH, at 2 mins, 34 secs.

4, Gilbert Duclos-Lasalle (FRA) Z-Peugeot, same time.

5, Jean-Claude Bagot (FRA) Fagor, same time.

6, Niki Ruttiman (SWI) Toshiba-Look, same time.

61, Kvetoslav Palov at 2 mins, 37 secs.

80, Steve Swart, same time.

134, Malcolm Elliott, same time.

143, Adrian Timmis, same time.

181, Shane Sutton, same time.

199, Guy Gallopin, at 30 mins, 33 secs.

Graham Jones, abandoned.

Paul Watson, abandoned.

Yellow jersey: Erich Maechler.

Stage 7: Épinal to Troyes, 211 kilometres, 41.066 kilometres an hour

Tuesday, July 7

Frenchman Régis Clère of the Spanish team Teka was keen to impress family, friends and neighbours in his home region of the Haute-Marne. After following the climbers over the third-category Côte du Bois de Bourmont, he attacked on the descent and set off on a lone foray into his own territory. With a £1,000 prize for the first rider to pass through the birthplace of Charles de Gaulle at

Colombey-les-deux-Églises perhaps Clère also had other motives, but the *peloton*, showing its traditional generosity to riders on home ground, allowed him his taste of glory before winding up the chase. By Colombey, Clère's lead (at one time 8 minutes) had dwindled to 10 seconds and after 60 miles Clère's spell in the limelight was over. Once across the Aube River the Frenchman had been enveloped and the attacks and counter-attacks on the way into Troyes began. First to show his face was Australian Phil Anderson of Panasonic, desperate to restore a faded reputation. Anderson twice struck out in a bid to rob the sprinters at the finish, followed by his team mate Allan Peiper in another lone breakaway. All efforts proved fruitless, however, and with 6 miles to go the teams began to jockey their speed merchants into position for the sprint. First to show were Van Poppel's Super Confex, who had worked like madmen over the fast run-in, but then Roche himself created a gap for the Carrera sprinter Guido Bontempi. Also up in a good position was ANC's Malcolm Elliott and he takes up the story: 'I was up alongside Kelly and Van Poppel at the last corner with 500 metres to go when there was a slight lull and Bontempi came past us like a train, knocking Kelly out of the way.'

Bontempi won easily from Manuel Jorge Domínguez of BH with a disappointed and angry Van Poppel third, although not as angry as the Super Confex manager Jan Raas, who had seen most of the team's hard work go to waste. 'Jan was furious at dinner that night,' said Van Poppel, who has no hesitation in nominating himself as the fastest sprinter in the world. 'He banged on the table and made it clear that he would not tolerate another mess-up like this.'

And Bontempi, the 27-year-old Italian, said modestly: 'These days you need some luck to win a sprint and that was the case today because both Super Confex and Joker were playing the game for their sprinter. Carrera's priority is to defend Maechler's jersey and look after any potential offensive from Stephen Roche.

My personal profit must come last. Today I followed the wheel of Stephen Roche, feeling good, until 300 metres from the line, then I went, without a glance behind. When I feel strong nothing stops me.'

Bontempi had shown the animal instincts of a true sprinter, although how much of this was in-born and how much artificially created remains unclear. The stage winner failed the routine dope test on traces of testosterone, the hormone which produces aggression, and was declassified.

1, Manuel Jorge Domínguez (SPA) BH, 5 hours, 8 mins, 17 secs.
2, Jean-Paul Van Poppel (NL) Super Confex, same time.
3, Josef Lieckens (BEL) Joker, same time.
4, Sean Kelly (IRE) Kas, same time.
5, Johan Capiot (BEL) Roland-Skala, same time.
6, Mathieu Hermans (NL) Caja Rural, same time.
9, Malcolm Elliott, same time.
32, Guy Gallopin, same time.
84, Adrian Timmis, same time.
107, Kvetoslav Palov, at 21 secs.
176, Shane Sutton, same time.
179, Steve Swart, same time.

Yellow jersey: Erich Maechler.

Stage 8: Troyes to Épinay-sous-Senart, 205.5 kilometres, 38.069 kilometres an hour

Wednesday, July 8

Raas, Super Confex and Van Poppel got it right next day on a stage highlighted by the second longest break of the Tour . . . from Colombia's Julio César Cadena. Cadena, making his Tour debut, went away from a completely uninterested *peloton* at 18 miles and hung on for another 88 before blowing up. On the road, the Colombian took three Catch sprints and on two occasions took overall race leadership from Maechler. Cadena was 10 minutes down on Maechler at the start of the day but, in between a hiccup in the middle where he seemed to tire, twice took his stage lead over the magic figure. Despite the efforts of his team mates, who tried to slow down the chase, the bunch's will proved the stronger and on a small rise in the village of Varenées-Jarcy, site of the stage's final Catch sprint, Cadena's dream of becoming the first Colombian in the Tour de France yellow jersey was over, helped by a derailed chain. The Catch prize was taken by Omar Palov of ANC, showing a healthy determination not to be overawed in this mighty company, and he was joined by five other riders in a potential winning break. No one seemed prepared to take control and organise, however, and by the time the race roared into the confined streets of the Paris suburb of Epinay-sous-Sénart, it was down to the sprinters again.

The last 400 yards along the Avenue Général Charles de Gaulle are slightly uphill. While a large group swayed and snarled along the right-hand barrier, Van Poppel took off up the left-hand rail alone to blaze a trail to victory. Belgians Michel Vermote and Johan Capiot came second and third, with another 188 riders credited with the same time behind. Three and a half minutes later Cadena, the lonely hero, wobbled over the line to sympathetic applause.

Said Van Poppel: 'We got it right today. Last night some of my team had indicated that they would not work for me again in the sprints but Jan Raas intervened. He recommended that we didn't start to surge until Carrera did and that lesson bore fruit.'

1, Jean-Paul Van Poppel (NL) Super Confex, 5 hours, 23 mins, 53 secs.

2, Michel Vermote (BEL) RMO, same time.

3, Johan Capiot (BEL) Roland-Skala, same time.

4, Bruno Wojtinek (FRA) Z-Peugeot, same time.

5, Josef Lieckens (BEL) Joker, same time.

6, Stefano Allocchio (ITAL) Supermercati, same time.

25, Malcolm Elliott, same time.

47, Kvetoslav Palov, same time.

105, Guy Gallopin, same time.

137, Adrian Timmis, same time.

188, Steve Swart, same time.

197, Shane Sutton, at 15 mins, 30 secs.

Yellow jersey: Erich Maechler.

Stage 9: Orléans to Renazé, 260 kilometres, 36.628 kilometres an hour

Thursday, July 9

The longest and dullest stage of the Tour came to life in the last 14 miles. With the thought of the individual time trial at Saumur to come the following day, the *peloton* were content to take things easy, with only the occasional Catch sprints to rouse the team car personnel and spectators from torpor. But with 160 rolling miles gone a group of five – Adrie Van Der Poel of Holland, Ludo Peeters of Belgium, Roberto Amadio of Italy, Theo De Rooy of Holland and Dominique Garde of France – escaped. The break looked half-hearted at first and had been whittled down to just over 1 minute when, with 8 miles left, a spectacular pile-up in the bunch gave them their second, unexpected chance. While the riders behind struggled to extricate themselves, the wily Peeters, 2 minutes 32 seconds behind the yellow jersey of Erich Maechler overnight, quickly realised that he could take overall race leadership if the break could build up a large enough gap. Peeters lost out in the sprint to Van Der Poel and Amadio while, behind, a chase organised by Carrera's Guido Bontempi had pulled the bunch back to 1½ minutes and Maechler kept his yellow jersey for one more night.

1, Adrie Van Der Poel (NL) PDM, 7 hours, 5 mins, 54 secs.
2, Roberto Amadio (ITAL) Supermercati, same time.
3, Ludo Peeters (BEL) Super Confex, same time.
4, Theo De Rooy (NL) Panasonic, same time.
5, Dominique Garde (FRA) Toshiba-Look, same time.
6, Guido Bontempi (ITAL) Carrera, at 1 min, 21 secs.
18, Malcolm Elliott, at 1 min, 32 secs.
24, Kvetoslav Palov, same time.
54, Guy Gallopin, same time.
62, Adrian Timmis, same time.
189, Steve Swart, same time.
197, Shane Sutton, at 3 mins, 56 secs.

Yellow jersey: Erich Maechler.

CHAPTER 5

TOUR DE FARCE

'You look a bit wasted, Jeff, a touch dehydrated,' said Steve Snowling as I hobbled slowly and painfully into the dining room of the Hotel Ibis in Poitiers.

I knew what he meant. Looking in the mirror in my room half an hour earlier I'd seen a pair of sunken cheeks and glassy eyes. There was a throbbing ache in the back of my neck, and my wrists and thighs burned. I had a raging thirst, and a raw sunburn, etched sharply by the outlines of a short-sleeved cycling jersey, contrasted sharply with the white wastes where the sun had refused to go. I had just spent the best part of a day pedalling 100 miles through rural rolling France and the experience had left its mark. The Tour's second time trial, 59 miles from Saumur close to Renazé to Futuroscope, a 21st-century theme park on the outskirts of Poitiers, was for most of the ANC team a journey into the unknown. Tests of this length are rare in Britain and most admitted they did not know what to expect.

If they were dreading it, so was I because this, I had reasoned, was my last chance of fulfilling the wishes of my employers and riding the length of a stage, however tentative and amateurish the effort would prove. In relative terms it was a short stage and with luck I might survive the experience, although I was facing an extra 40 miles from Angers, our overnight stop, to Saumur, and from Futuroscope to our hotel in Poitiers at the other end.

Snowling and the other two mechanics had worked past midnight in Angers, first washing the caked grime from six bikes after the 175 miles from Orléans on the race's longest stage and then tuning the bikes for the individual riders ready for the time trial. All the while they were chivvied and harried by Griffiths, who paced up and down the hotel garage like a regimental sergeant major, demanding this change or that change.

He and Snowling had become involved in a long and protracted argument over seat adjustments for Timmis, while Capper and Fisher, the laymen, hovered impotently on the fringe.

'Adrian has got a very long back,' said Griffiths, 'you'll have to move his saddle back a centimetre.'

Snowling was equally adamant that he had got it right and the contretemps blew over with him telling the team director: 'I didn't get this job just by blowing up tyres, you know.'

Professional cyclists' bikes are tailor-made but Snowling and Griffiths had agreed that I could borrow Watson's spare, although I was a good five inches taller than the departed climber. I was impressed if a little alarmed by their faith as they handed over the ultra-light £1,000 machine complete with 14 gears. Armed with a *bidon* full of water, a *musette* containing a map of the area, route profile and some spare food as well as some small change, I donned the black Lycra, chamois-padded shorts and a short-sleeved jersey and prepared to set out. At the last minute Snowling ran over to strap a spare tube under the seat, although if I punctured I hadn't a clue how to do a change and the tube was really there as a psychological prop.

Taking care that none of the riders saw me I wheeled off into the unknown. The first problem was to get out of Angers and away from its traffic, and after a few wobbling attempts to read the map on the move I decided to ask.

'*Pardon, monsieur, la route à Poitiers, s'il vous plaît?*' I asked a middle-aged Frenchman at the first set of red lights. Before he could reply I toppled slowly over sideways on to the pavement, unable to free my trainers from the pedal clips and put my legs down on the road.

Phil Griffiths had told me that you're not a cyclist until you've had a fall but as I hit the pavement, landing painfully on the point of an elbow, I considered this a somewhat hasty baptism. I'd travelled less than a mile.

Between laughing fits the Frenchman pointed me on the right road and I headed gratefully off into the Loire plain towards the fields of yellow sunflowers and the shimmering heat of the distant horizon.

The stage route was out of bounds of course, but I'd worked out a parallel version of a roughly similar length and degree of difficulty and I was due to join the Tour stretch at Loudun, the feeding point where, if they hadn't all gone through by then, I would be able to catch a view of the time trial. At first all went well and I cruised along in a big gear enjoying the day and with occasional experiments with the *bidon* and map. But when I tried squeezing some water from the plastic bottle into my mouth I invariably missed and it splashed all over my face. Taking one hand off the handlebars to look at the map precipitated a heartwrenching wobble into the paths of the juggernauts steaming outside me down the D748.

As the miles slowly passed and the gradients and headwind increased, so the gears went lower and lower. Once I dialled the wrong number and the chain came off altogether.

Before long I found myself shifting around the saddle as the tissues in my backside, unused to this prolonged abuse, began to compress and complain. By the time I'd pedalled into Loudun and gratefully sunk onto a straw bale alongside Friedhelm, my respect for professional cyclists had increased tenfold.

The big German, there to feed ANC on the way through, was greatly amused. His ordeal was yet to come, little did he know.

At intervals the riders flashed through, trailed by a lone team car, some looking elegant, others stomping fiercely on the pedals in red-faced effort. ANC's last man was Elliott and it had been planned that Capper, who was following, would pick up Friedhelm and his ice box to take him to the finish.

But as Capper pulled up and Friedhelm prepared to climb in, the team manger suddenly shouted: 'No, no, not in here', waved him away and motored on. Friedhelm was dumbfounded. He was stranded in mid-stage with the finish line and his hotel 25 miles away.

Friedhelm picked up his ice box and, muttering in disgust, set off to walk. I wheeled off again towards Poitiers, pedalling in an obscene parody of the Tour stylists like Roche who had whirred through moments earlier, his head straight, mouth open in the familiar snarl and hardly deviating off line as he rode towards the day's victory. It was a picture for the connoisseur.

The last 20 miles passed in a haze of tortured discomfort. The sound of the traffic seemed to become more distant as the energy and willpower slipped away and when I stopped at a roadside café the temptation to ask if they had any rooms overnight was almost overpowering.

The final hill into Poitiers saw me off the bike and walking, although I climbed hastily back aboard when I saw the ANC-Halfords insignia on the Citroën parked outside a chemist's. It was Sabino, who looked at me in a mixture of horror and pity.

'How far's the hotel?' I croaked.

'Still 3 kilometres,' said the *soigneur*.

I willed him to offer me a lift, take the bike off me, bolt it to the Citroën roof and transport me to the journey's end. But he wouldn't and pride wouldn't let me ask. On my last legs I rode into the hotel drive. My first and last long-distance bike ride was mercifully over.

'Friedhelm's got third-degree burns,' chortled Griffiths at dinner. The 17-stone German had walked with his ice box almost to the outskirts of Poitiers in broiling heat until he had been picked up by Jan Raas, manager of the Dutch Super Confex team. He had refused to come down to dinner, staying in his room and preparing the riders' food for the next day.

'He's not angry,' said Snowling. 'He just feels humiliated. Raas couldn't believe that a team would leave one of its *soigneurs* like that.'

And when Capper appeared to eat Snowling said with ill-concealed sarcasm: 'In case you're interested, Friedhelm's back.'

'OK, OK, it was a mistake,' said the team manager. 'Just a hiccup in the organisation; he'll come round.'

One of the French TV channels was showing an X-rated movie and Sabino was scuttling round the lobby and dining room with his eyes shining.

'I'm pissed off with him,' said Angus. 'He's done nothing and thinks he knows everything. I am the *chef* round here and people do what I say.'

Riders and personnel stopped eating in amazement as the Scotsman thumped the table. 'If I tell them, even the waiters will change their trousers.' With that, Fraser clambered to his feet and stormed out. Perhaps the pressures were getting to everybody.

From Poitiers the race headed south to Chaumeil in another long stage of 170 miles. Shane was struggling again, finishing over half an hour behind the winner, and both he and Capper had been fined a total of 1,100 francs for prolonged pushing and pacing, but Gallopin his room mate seemed to have found a new lease of life. At the ancient Hôtel Bon Accueil in Tulle, site of ANC's overnight stop, the Frenchman walked into the bar where I'd set up 'office' and accepted a glass of wine.

Gallopin, short, stocky and strong as a bull, looks like everyone's idea of a professional commando, an impression reinforced by his fighting spirit. But this hard man also had heart.

This was his sixth Tour and the only one he'd missed was in 1982 when his father had died. He missed his father, '*un vrai gentilhomme*'.

'When I began cycling he helped and encouraged me, always there at the finish with a bottle. I have four brothers who also ride and he encouraged us all, a very sporting family.'

On Stage 6, from Strasbourg, where only Griffiths' tows pulled him through, Guy admitted he had nearly climbed off his bike and abandoned the race.

'I was in a bad state, but I came out of it . . . with some help, of course,' he grinned.

'What made you carry on, then?' I asked.

'My duties to the team of course. And we were also close to my home in the next days and my wife was to come and see me go past. Also I recalled my misadventures in 1983 when I had no morale at all. My wife was in hospital and I did the whole Alpine stage of Morzine just in front of the broom wagon. From start to finish I did not see another rider. Except of course the 35 who had already been picked up by the broom wagon!

'This Tour I've had a chest infection since Berlin. Jones, Watson and Chesneau, I believe, had the same complaint, but I'm still here and they are gone. That's not bad.'

What did he think of the ANC team?

'They are some of the best English riders and I think some could sign contracts with Continental teams next year . . . if that has not already happened in the case of Adrian Timmis. He is very good, a future leader and I would be very surprised if a *directeur sportif* with some vision did not engage him because he reminds me of Roche and Kelly.'

With that ANC's Frenchman rose to his feet.

'Now I must retire,' said Gallopin. I raised my glass: 'To Paris.'

There was a long pause, then, in English: 'I 'ope so.'

Stage 10: Saumur to Futuroscope individual time trial, 87.5 kilometres, 44.442 kilometres an hour

Friday, July 10

The ultra-long 59-mile time trial from Saumur was thought to be a good indicator of the potential winning form of Tour favourites like Roche, and so it proved. Roche won by 42 seconds from the new yellow jersey Charly Mottet and jumped to sixth overall, but the day proved a drastic disappointment for his countryman Sean Kelly, who many had predicted would begin his surge up the overall classification. Kelly finished 5 minutes down on Roche on the day and 10 minutes behind Mottet overall.

'I just haven't ridden enough in the last few weeks,' said Kelly. 'It was my legs that were a problem.'

Also disappointing was two-time Tour winner Laurent Fignon, who could only finish 20th on a course on which many thought he would excel, while climbers Robert Millar (11th) and Pedro Delgado (10th) surprised everyone.

Roche had predicted the night before that with a reasonable performance in the trial Mottet would take the yellow jersey, and he was right. The Frenchman finished a fine second behind the Irishman, with the tall thin Dane Jesper Skibby of Belgium's Roland-Skala team a surprise third. The bravest performance came from the Mexican, Alcalá, who crashed with 2 miles left, bending the frame of his bike, spraining a finger and sustaining head wounds that later required stitches. He still got up to finish – on a spare bike.

Roche was still trying to avoid thinking of the yellow jersey. 'So far Mottet has hidden in the *peloton*. He's small so it's easy to do for him. But now he's a bit more noticeable in yellow. Let's see how he takes the pressure.'

1, Stephen Roche (IRE) Carrera, 1 hour, 58 mins, 11 secs.

2, Charly Mottet (FRA) Système U, 42 secs behind.

3, Jesper Skibby (DEN) Roland-Skala, at 53 secs.

4, Marc Madiot (FRA) Système U, at 1 min, 9 secs.

5, Didi Thurau (WG) Roland-Skala, at 1 min, 20 secs.

6, Jean-François Bernard (FRA) Toshiba-Look, at 1 min, 24 secs.

49, Steve Swart, at 6 mins, 28 secs.

56, Malcolm Elliott, at 6 mins, 56 secs.

67, Adrian Timmis, at 8 mins, 16 secs.

87, Guy Gallopin, at 9 mins, 39 secs.

139, Kvetoslav Palov, at 13 mins, 7 secs.

179, Shane Sutton, at 16 mins, 28 secs.

Yellow jersey: Charly Mottet.

Stage 11: Poitiers to Chaumeil, 255 kilometres, 35.838 kilometres an hour

Saturday, July 11

Mottet's spell in yellow lasted one day – although he was soon to claim it back. His countryman and Système U team mate Martial Gayant, the French cyclocross champion, took this, the race's second longest stage, with ease. Gayant was away in a break of 10 that reached the outskirts of Chaumeil with a lead of over 11 minutes and on the long climb to the finish the Frenchman surged to cross the line 38 seconds ahead of Laudelino Cubino of Spain, the only rider to give any measure of chase. By then the main bunch of riders had decided that with the Pyrenees only a day away they would save what energy they had left and arrived in Chaumeil in a long line of threes and fours with Mottet glad to lose the burden of yellow jersey.

1, Martial Gayant (FRA) Système U, 7 hours, 6 mins, 55 secs.

2, Laudelino Cubino (SPA) BH, 38 secs behind.

3, Kim Andersen (DAN) Toshiba-Look, at 1 min, 38 secs.

4, Gilles Mas (FRA) RMO, at 1 min, 44 secs.

5, Massimo Ghirotto (ITAL) Carrera, at 3 mins, 27 secs.

6, Peter Hilse (WG) Teka, same time.

36, Adrian Timmis, at 11 mins, 2 secs.

124, Kvetoslav Palov, at 12 mins, 27 secs.

132, Malcolm Elliott, at 12 mins, 51 secs.

133, Guy Gallopin, at 13 mins, 7 secs.

154, Steve Swart, at 14 mins, 39 secs.

187, Shane Sutton, at 32 mins, 3 secs.

Yellow jersey: Martial Gayant.

CHAPTER 6

THE BIG BOSS

TONY CAPPER HAD BEEN IN his time a policeman, a taxi driver, a managing director and a millionaire. Now he was a team manager in the greatest bike race in the world. He loved it. He loved the limelight, the interviews and the press coverage back home. He loved being in charge, making the decisions, controlling the budget and the daily lives of the riders. And he loved the driving in a situation where normal rules of the road didn't apply. His favoured trick was to fall behind the convoy towards the end of a stage to buy an ice cream and then speed flat out in chase, tearing down mountain roads in a squeal of brakes and burning rubber and blasting his horn on the way through villages. On one stage he had become involved in a dust-up with the driver of the Z-Peugeot lead car, with each determined that the next place in the long line was theirs. Locked together like the chariots in *Ben-Hur* we flew down the middle of the road with the drivers cursing each other in their respective languages until a tree-lined island finally parted them.

'That showed him,' scoffed our leader.

* * *

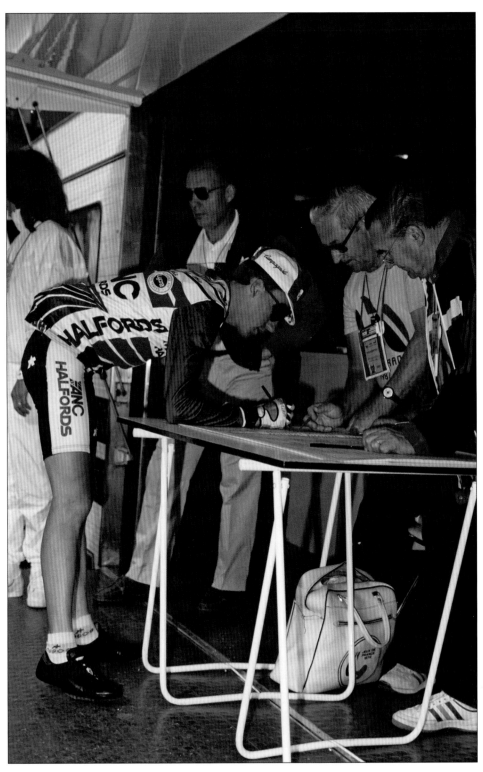

Adrian Timmis signs on for the 1987 Tour de France. He would develop into a mature professional cyclist over the course of the race. (© Phil O'Connor)

Graham Jones, one of Britain's best-ever cyclists and easily the most experienced on the ANC-Halfords team. (© Phil O'Connor)

Australian Shane Sutton gets ready to begin his Berlin prologue effort. (© Phil O'Connor)

Bernard Chesneau leads Guy Gallopin as the two Frenchmen battle it out in the Berlin team time trial. (© Phil O'Connor)

Steve Swart and Kvetoslav Palov before the Berlin time trial. (© Phil O'Connor)

Tony Capper, ANC-Halfords team manager, in Berlin at
the start of the first stage. (© Phil O'Connor)

The ANC-Halfords team begin their 1987 Tour de France, the first British team to enter the race in 20 years. (© Phil O'Connor)

Malcolm Elliott (l), ANC-Halfords team leader, and Adrian Timmis
fight their way up l'Alpe d'Huez. (© Phil O'Connor)

Guy Gallopin on l'Alpe d'Huez. (© Phil O'Connor)

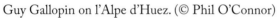

Stephen Roche, 1987 Tour de France winner with Jeannie Longo,
Tour Féminin winner, celebrating on the Champs-Elysées. (© Phil O'Connor)

Capper was a good, fast driver, if a trifle extrovert, and for a big man showed remarkable stamina through long hot days, particularly in a stifling saloon where he would never allow the sun roof to be opened for fear of burning his bald head.

With his 20-stone bulk squeezed into the front of the Peugeot and with the team's short-wave radio (which invariably never worked) by his side along with his 'press relations manager' Donald Fisher, for whom Capper could do no wrong, the team manager piloted his charges around France. For their own reasons, Griffiths, Snowling and Fraser, the leaders of the ANC teams within a team, seldom had a good word to say about him, although one thing they would all have to admit: Capper, through all the tribulations and diverse daily problems of the race, never once panicked.

At Tulle, squashed under an umbrella on the boulevard and drinking wine I had bought him and smoking cigarettes I had paid for – like most rich men from working-class backgrounds Capper was very careful with his pennies – he gave his mid-race report.

With three of his riders gone already, I asked the ANC team manager whether he had lowered his sights.

'No, not really. I think we are still entitled to a stage win from one or two riders and we are probably there with a dark horse and that's Guy. I think he's been able to suffer the two days' illness, get through it and regain his strength – we were coming up the last climb today and having seen him on the first three days we were sort of looking up and saying the next guy around the corner is going to be Guy but there he was in the second group behind the main bunch. In the last four days he's never been out of the action. That takes a special sort of genius who won't give in, so in fact Guy has been a revelation. I was a bit disappointed with him earlier in the season but he's totally changed my view of him in the last ten days – you know, I admit my admiration for him as I do with Shane.

'Guy would make a good Welsh miner, he'd make a superb blacksmith, he'd make a good bosun's mate – he's that kind of man, hard as bloody nails and I'd like to think, in fact there's a strong possibility, that in a few years Guy will be our Continental *directeur sportif* and you couldn't wish for a better man to have as a number two on the team.

'I think the rest of the team have shown all the character we thought possible from them; in no way have we been disappointed.

'Malcolm saw himself as a rider and as a rider believed in himself. If you'd seen Malcolm two years ago you'd have been justified in raising a question about his discipline but he's certainly changed very very rapidly. But we don't want to switch him off, so you don't say to a child who's been allowed sweets once a day for the last two years "Tomorrow you're not getting any more." You may be able to say you're only going to get them three times a week and in a year's time you've got to get them down to once a week. OK, Malcolm's the team leader and feels he has to act pissed off from time to time, but he's all right.

'Adrian Timmis is quite possibly the first British Tour de France winner if we can avoid putting too much pressure on him. I think if we pressurised him he would crack because I think he's the sort of lad who would go eyeballs out if you told him to ride within himself.'

Could he see a conflict between Elliott and Timmis in a team?

'No, they are totally different riders. One is a sprinter who will get in there and mix it with them, an attacking rider in terms of the flat, faster stages. Malcolm's the kind of bloke like Kelly who can take punches in the Tour. De Gribaldy, the guy who signed Kelly from Ireland, said Elliott is the next Kelly and that was in front of a roomful of 18 people. Timmis is the smooth, stylish sort of rider, the sort who will be in there at the top of the climbs and the type who will be in there at, shall we say, the death?

'What we do lack in terms of the Tour is an out-and-out time triallist and we need another pure climber rather than an all-rounder like Adrian.'

What about the rest of the personnel, the *soigneurs* and mechanics?

'It's been a little bit of a shoestring. Instead of having the people we would like, such as full-time mechanics for the year, which is totally justified in terms of what it would cost, we've had to say: "Will you come for this race or will you come for that race?" As a result there's been a bit of a lack of discipline. That's got to be put right.

'Exactly the same with the masseurs. We need a full-time contracted masseur who is responsible for bringing in more when required. Then it's his responsibility and there's no question of people coming in and saying: "Hey, I'm number one." That's up to the bloke who's employed them, because it's part of his budget. They know they're quite clear they go to Angus first to be paid and it's no good them arguing they're a better masseur than Angus because he's paying them out.'

Capper broke off – he'd just spotted Sabino walking past with his brother.

'Hey, Sabino, are you into these young boys then?' asked the big boss, showing his cruder side.

'Where was I? Yeah, we've got Angus for this period of time because he was our first choice and he's the best *soigneur* in Britain and probably the only one who can be compared to a Continental one. It's his technical knowledge – you'll have to bear with me on the names of the, y'know, electrodes – he's fully qualified on that. He's a fully qualified masseur, he's a qualified physiotherapist and he knows sports medicine, so that he's able to recognise troubles with a rider, give advice and be able to put them right in terms of diet, exercise and things like that.

'His problem is that he's got two *soigneurs* he personally wouldn't have picked and of course that gives him every opportunity to say: "I don't agree with this or that."

'OK, he's a bit of a moaner but he's the best in Britain. He can tell a rider what's wrong with him and that rider will bloody well believe him. Now if I stand there and say: "You've got a cold", he would almost certainly go and ask Angus and he'd tell him: "You've got a little minor touch of influenza." As for the mechanics, they of course are another team, and they're totally on their own.'

Having seen the mechanics work up to 15 hours a day without noticeable appreciation, I asked Capper if he thought they got the credit they deserve.

'Yes, at the end of the day the credit they deserve is the willingness of a rider to trust himself totally to a bike that's been done by a mechanic, when the rider is prepared to take his hands off the brakes at 70 or 80 kilometres an hour down a mountainside. Really, as a mechanic, he's got no right to ask for anyone to compliment him. But they do get acknowledged in a way that's perhaps not immediately evident, and if we say we want mechanics for a certain race the riders are very quick to turn round and say: "Hang on, we want Steve – what's his name – Steve Snowling" because they know if Steve Snowling does the job it's going to be done properly.

'The difficulties we've had have been more in personality than actually doing the job.

'The instances where the riders have suffered because of any difficulties, or maybe differences is a better word, have been very few and far between. Only once have we had problems with a race start in terms of equipment being there, only once in the whole race to date. Not once have we had problems in terms of timing or anything else – and the whole thing is totally uncontrollable by us. It was imposed on us by the organisation and it was problems after a race in terms of picking people up.

'We had a little bit of a communication problem on one occasion when we should have had a vehicle down for servicing, but again this is not a mistake we'll make again because the instant it happened an instruction was given to all people concerned that the radios should stay on after the race.

'In terms of organisation we're not even in the top ten in terms of the Tour but I think next year we can look at ourselves and say, organisationally, we are in the top ten because we can organise well. The number of hiccups that we haven't solved I could count on the fingers of one hand in a whole year. We're talking about two or three occasions and they've been solved instantly.

'Success to me is not not making mistakes but is recognising them when you make them and correcting them.

'Because anyone who thinks they can do summat and not make mistakes is a fool.'

Next morning, while Friedhelm smothered his sunburn in Calamine, Sabino found himself in trouble again. He'd forgotten to pick the *bidons* up from race headquarters and Capper was ranting at him in fury. The little Frenchman cowered like a puppy that had just been slippered, unable to understand what he'd done wrong.

Looking up to the first-floor window where the riders were preparing for Stage 12 from Brive to Bordeaux I could see Malcolm Elliott framed in the window, his face a picture of blissful glee as the personnel swore and shouted in the street below.

While Capper raged at Sabino, the little *soigneur*'s brother a few kilometres down the road in the Kas hotel was slapping and kneading the leg muscles of the world's No. 1 bike rider into condition for the 154-mile stage. Sean Kelly, Freeman of Waterford, the most famous citizen of Co. Tipperary and Ireland's greatest sporting hero, was off to the wars. It was to be his last day on the 1987 Tour.

CHAPTER 7

THE IRISH ROVERS

SPREADEAGLED ACROSS ONE OF THE Kas team's Peugeots, calf muscles flattened alarmingly across the car bonnet and face set hard against the world, Sean Kelly looked a mean man indeed.

While a large jostling crowd of TV cameras, microphone booms and notebooks across the town square showed the whereabouts of his friend and countryman, Stephen Roche, Kelly – christened John but called Sean in the family home to avoid confusion with his father – kept three feet of space between himself and the rest of the human race.

Roche was going through the pre-stage ritual of quote and unquote, answering in fluent French, English or Italian, always with a courteous smile. Roche had worked out long ago that with the press on your side half your battles as a professional sportsman were won, and indeed regarded these hurly-burly impromptu press conferences as part of his duty to team and sponsor. Even in Italy when the crowds were baying for his blood he remained, on the surface at least, affable, never refusing an autograph or failing to respond to a question.

Kelly, the rough-hewn farmer's son from Carrick-on-Suir on

the boundary between Tipperary and Waterford, could manage without fans and journalists very nicely, thank you.

Kelly had spent 11 years as a professional cyclist. He'd won his first race, a handicap with Carrick Wheelers, in his home town at 14, became Irish junior champion and in 1975 produced a winning sprint to take the Sheffield stage of the Round Britain Milk Race. However, his victory produced a hint of the Irishman's obdurate nature when second-placed Swede Bernt Johansson, livid that Kelly had sat on his wheel for most of the winning break, confronted Kelly at the stage end. As Johansson ranted at the young opportunist, Kelly, always economic with words, replied simply: 'Fuck off.' The Swede had become the first of many to sample Kelly's lack of compromise . . . on and off a bicycle.

At the time, Kelly was making a living as a bricklayer between spells of work on his father's farm at Curraghduff in Carrick-on-Suir and had hardly considered a professional cycling career. But when he was banned from the Montreal Games of 1976 by the International Olympic Committee for competing in South Africa, the die was cast and at the age of 20 Kelly signed a contract for £6,000 a year to ride as a *domestique* for Jean de Gribaldy, *directeur sportif* of the Continental team Flandria, with squads based both in France and Belgium.

Working for Freddy Maertens, the then world champion, Kelly had little chance to impress, slaving away in the service of the team leader, fetching for him, carrying for him, even towing him up hills on occasions. But already there were signs that the taciturn foreigner was cut out for something more glamorous than the life of a beast of burden. In 1978, at the age of 22 and on his race debut, Kelly took the sprint into Poitiers and his first stage victory in the Tour de France.

It was to be the first of five Kelly stage wins in the Tour but his rough-house, no-holds-barred style in the finishing straight was also to earn him some notoriety among his fellow riders. Twice he was demoted for 'irregularities' when rivals who happened to get in the way on his way to the line were unceremoniously barged aside.

The Poitiers win increased Kelly's market value and by next year he was riding, at a salary that had trebled virtually overnight, for the Belgian Splendor team, basing himself in Vilvoorde, north of Brussels, learning Flemish and setting down roots. Even when he returned to de Gribaldy and his Sem France Loire team in 1982 and later his present team Kas, Kelly continued to live in Belgium . . . when not travelling around Europe on two wheels for ten or more months of the year. Today, like Glaswegian Robert Millar, who is also based in Belgium, Kelly's native brogue competes with the nasal patois of Flemish when he talks.

When he talks. Amid all this Kelly is said to have remained Kelly – close, shy, suspicious of strangers and sometimes of acquaintances and still very economic with words. Des Cahill had told me that Kelly was the only man who nodded in answer to questions in a radio interview and there was the tale of the journalist who, anxious to get an insight into the great man, had decided to spend a whole day in his car journeying to a race. Kelly is alleged to have addressed the journalist twice during the day . . . once to say hello and once to say goodbye.

So there he was on the Kas Peugeot, head down and willing outsiders to keep away. Journalistic duty told me I had to go over and talk to Kelly but for the first time in my career I was terrified of approaching a sports personality (the reporter's usual philosophy is that they can only tell you to go away once). Des had told me that Kelly could spot a 'civilian' (someone who knew nothing about cycling) within seconds and usually reacted accordingly. So I hung back, watching Kelly out of the corner of my eye and desperately trying to summon up the courage to go over and be told to go away . . . or worse.

Geoff Shergold, the ANC mechanic, had no such qualms.

'I once beat Sean Kelly, you know,' he said. 'It was in the GS Europa two-day event in Southampton and I outsprinted him. It was his first race outside Ireland. He was 15 at the time.

'I tell you what, I wonder if he remembers. I'll go over and ask him.'

'But, Geoff, he looks in a real mean mood and he might not appreciate it just before the start of a stage.'

As I spoke, I watched a middle-aged French cycling fan, who had somehow infiltrated the police cordon around the square, approach Kelly hopefully holding a pencil and a grubby piece of paper.

Kelly said nothing, just petrified the man with a long continuous stare until the hapless autograph hunter retreated in confusion.

'See what I mean?' I asked Shergold. 'Did you see how he reacted to that guy?'

'Oh, that's all right, he just got the approach wrong. He can only tell me to go away anyway. Here, I tell you what, you take a picture of us.' The mechanic pushed a camera into my hand.

This was very worrying. If Kelly took it the wrong way and decided that this constituted an invasion of privacy, I was implicated. Perhaps he'd never speak to me.

Standing at a safe distance I watched as Shergold approached the aggressive-looking figure in the blue and yellow Kas jersey. I could see Shergold talking animatedly and watched Kelly's impassive reaction. Any minute now . . . I got ready to disown Shergold and his camera when to my amazement a huge grin cracked Kelly's face, he took Shergold's proffered hand and turned towards the camera to pose with the man who had outsprinted him 16 years earlier.

'You see, he remembered,' said a delighted Shergold on his return.

Perhaps Kelly wasn't as bad as the dour legend and when a few minutes later he agreed to pose with one of the condom publicity people, holding a packet up for the camera and saying: 'Don't whatever you do tell them about this back in Carrick!', all my earlier fears vanished.

'Excuse me, Mr Kelly, I wonder if you could spare me a few minutes. My name's Jeff Connor and I work for the Star newspaper in Manchester . . .'

Kelly said nothing, climbed slowly off the car bonnet on to his bike, pulled his gloves on tighter and, without even looking at me, rode slowly away.

'*Chute au kilometre 57,*' announced the impassive tones of Radio Tour. We were motoring along close to the banks of the Dordogne on the way to Bordeaux on Stage 12 when it happened. In the tangle of riders and stampede of cameramen and mechanics to the scene there was total confusion. When the dust cleared, the *peloton* disappeared up the road leaving a lone, grimacing figure behind. It was Kelly.

The year 1987 hadn't been a good one for the Irish superstar. He had been dogged by bad luck in the early season classics – he had twice crashed in Paris–Roubaix; he had looked like finding form and good fortune in the Tour of Spain when he held the yellow jersey, until he was forced to abandon by an unglamorous but extremely painful boil on the backside. Nor had the Tour de France gone much better – he had disappointed in the two time trials and lost out in the sprints. His fall on the road to Bordeaux seemed an inevitable and premature climax to a year of frustration.

Kelly climbed slowly back on his bike after a long minute clutching his left shoulder and, after first setting off in the wrong direction, reorientated himself and pedalled slowly and painfully after the race. Two Kas team mates had hung back and, one on either side, pushed their leader along until race director Jacques Goddet intervened, telling them: 'I'm sorry, but that is not allowed.'

Stephen Roche, his great friend, came back off the bunch to

see how his countryman was and reported to the *peloton*: 'He doesn't know where he is.'

The accident produced a temporary truce to the day's racing. 'We just rode along for 10 miles dead slow,' said ANC's Shane Sutton. 'It was sickening.' Kelly suffered on for another 12 miles before a small hill stopped him in his tracks. There he climbed slowly off his bike and, finally realising that his Tour was over, fell weeping into the arms of his *directeur sportif*. 'This has definitely not been my year,' he said.

It most definitely was the year for Stephen Roche. After his hard-earned triumph in the Tour of Italy, the Dubliner had climbed for the first time out of the giant shadow of his idol and countryman Kelly, and when the Tour set off from Berlin he had found himself, not too willingly, one of the big favourites to take cycling's greatest classic.

At stage starts Roche found himself the centre of attention from the media, conducting interviews in French and English, invariably with the easy Irish grace that made him so popular not just with journalists, who found his reading of races an excellent source of copy, but also with the French fans.

They had decided that next to a Frenchman winning their Tour, a Gaelic charmer married to an attractive French girl and with a home close to Paris would be the next best thing.

The smile and the charm, however, hide the instincts of a predator. In the dog eat dog world of professional cycling there isn't a great future in being a losing Mr Nice Guy.

In Italy Roche had admitted that if the Visentini fans had brought him down he would have endeavoured to take the Italian with him. Roche was to show a similar, if less extreme, competitive ruthlessness on his way to Tour de France triumph, systematically eliminating his main rivals one by one until by the last day in the Alps only Pedro Delgado of Spain was left.

* * *

Roche, like so many riders, looks puny and fragile away from his bike. He was brought up in Dundrum, a working-class suburb of Dublin between the Wicklow Mountains and the sea. His father, who still lives in Dundrum close to a small semi-detached his son also maintains there, was a milkman and Roche as a youngster would be out on the round at five in the morning carrying bottles for 'Da'.

It was Roche Senior who insisted that Stephen finished his four-year apprenticeship as a fitter and welder. Although a successful amateur, Roche admits he had given little thought to cycling as a career. Selected for Ireland in the Moscow Olympics of 1980, Roche had travelled over to Paris for the first time to prepare. After a disagreement with his coach over training (for all the geniality, Roche's career is littered with dispute), he dropped out of the Irish squad to join the Peugeot ACCB amateur team in Paris. There he followed Graham Jones to the amateur points championship of France and by the end of the year had signed professional forms with Peugeot for the 1981 season to begin a spectacular climb to the top.

Three years with Peugeot culminated in more bitterness when the company sued him for moving to La Redoute after allegedly re-signing for them. When La Redoute withdrew their sponsorship, Roche found himself on the way to Italy and £200,000 a year from Carrera.

Through all this Roche on the bike had what he would call 'the usual ups and downs' – victory in the Paris–Nice in the first month of his pro career, third place in the 1985 Tour de France, a spectacular crash followed by knee surgery after the Paris six-day race in 1985, and the astonishing and eventful win in the Tour of Italy. But 1987 was mainly ups.

Roche is considered a lone wolf in the cycling fraternity, particularly after taking off to win in Italy against the orders of his team manager, but he would be first to admit that his 1987 successes would not have been possible without 'Team Roche' . . . his mechanic and masseur Patrick Valke and his *domestique*, Belgian rider Eddy Schepers. Where Roche went, so did they. When Carrera wanted to sack Schepers in 1986, Roche had demanded that he stay, and when he signed the 1988 contract with Fagor he had insisted they contract Schepers. What's more, part of the same deal was that Valke went along . . . as *directeur sportif*.

Both Schepers and Valke stuck with him through the trials of Italy when the Carrera management were ready to send them home. And when the showdown came with Delgado in the Alps in the Tour de France it was some remarkable, supercharged work from Schepers that kept Roche in contention when the Spanish climber was threatening to ride away to victory.

Schepers and Valke also served as a much-needed buffer for their boss when the media pressure became unbearable, as it inevitably did the closer Roche got to the yellow jersey.

Schepers, who roomed with the Irishman, was not averse to throwing over-inquisitive pressmen out of the bedroom and Valke could always be approached for a 'quote' if Roche for one reason or another wasn't available.

Most of the time, though, Roche was available. Perhaps too available for his own good.

Roche's easy and polite nature made him a natural target for the media. It was alarming to see him finish a stage after seven hard hours of racing and the hordes descend on him, pushing, pulling and punching to get the first questions in, even though one was a part of the same horde.

At Futuroscope, in the time trial that gave Roche his only stage win, one journalist couldn't even wait until Roche had stopped, leaping out into his path just over the finish line, causing the rider to brake so hard he almost flew over the handlebars.

No other sport and no other professional athlete would tolerate this. At Wimbledon or Lord's, players are allowed to shower and change and quench their thirst before returning to properly organised press conferences. On the Tour, the leaders are expected to stand sweat-stained and hungry, grimy and weary and go through the tactical nuances of the day's racing. The different TV and radio stations would want to get Roche in a corner alone for their own exclusive interviews – even though, inevitably, he could only repeat what he had said to the last man – while the newspaper journalists would queue in his hotel lobby for their few minutes with the tired rider. Little wonder the top men don't like the label of Tour favourite and will do their best to deflect the weighty title on to another's shoulders. The worst pressure doesn't come from their rivals.

By the time the Tour reached Bordeaux and headed south to the Pyrenees most riders were feeling the effects of the constant fast pace with attacks and chases each day and nobody in the pack taking charge and bringing some sense of order.

As Elliott succinctly put it: 'I'm shagged, absolutely shagged.'

Stage 12: Brive-la-Gaillarde to Bordeaux, 228 kilometres, 39.947 kilometres an hour

Sunday, July 12

After Kelly's accident and withdrawal, the *peloton* again raced conservatively, until the last 15 miles when Phil Anderson and six others got away to build up a 2-minute lead. But the workhorses of Super Confex again gave chase in the cause of Van Poppel and on the finishing loop of Bordeaux the sprinters were massing again – among them Malcolm Elliott of ANC and Davis Phinney of America's 7-Eleven team. On the last bend Teun Van Vliet of Panasonic swerved wide and Michel Vermote touched his rear wheel and went sprawling, bringing down several riders. The crash left Phinney in the clear – although he seemed to have Van Poppel beaten – and the American crossed the line overjoyed at another Tour de France stage to go with his third-stage win in the 1986 Tour.

'I heard the crash behind,' said the American later, 'but by then I was gone.' Although Elliott had been forced wide by the spill, he was finishing speedily enough to claim later that, but for the accident, he could have won. Vermote picked himself up painfully from the tarmac to finish (crashed riders can't be eliminated in the last kilometre) and the sprinters left centre stage to make way for the climbers and the first stage in the mountains. 'It's time for me to cause some disorder,' pledged the Colombian mountain king Luis Herrera.

1, Davis Phinney (US) 7-Eleven, 5 hours, 46 mins, 21 secs.
2, Jean-Paul Van Poppel (NL) Super Confex, same time.
3, Malcolm Elliott (GB) ANC, same time.
4, Jean Philippe Van Den Brande (BEL) Hitachi, same time.
5, Teun Van Vliet (NL) Panasonic, same time.
6, Marc Sergeant (BEL) Joker, same time.
120, Kvetoslav Palov, same time.

136, Adrian Timmis, same time.

156, Guy Gallopin, same time.

176, Steve Swart, same time.

187, Shane Sutton, 2 mins, 16 secs behind.

Yellow jersey: Martial Gayant.

CHAPTER 8

AND SOME YOU LOSE

BY STAGE 13 AND THE first sight of the Pyrenees Shane Sutton's Tour was moving inexorably and mercifully towards a close.

Every day, from the opening time trial around West Berlin, where he had been almost caught and passed by the rider behind, had brought some fresh form of trial and torture. His chirpy Aussie humour, which had made him more human alongside some of his dourer team mates, had long vanished. Traumatised by the fierce race pace, and with any ambition of helping the team buried, Shane had rationalised each day into simple survival, riding flat out with the peleton as long as possible and then, safe in the knowledge that he was inside the time limit for the day, sitting up in the saddle and desperately trying to save some energy for his next session on the rack.

It was a way of earning a living that wouldn't appeal to many and Shane's mental state was not improved by the constant fear that perhaps, in fact, it wasn't earning him a living. A phone call home to his wife had revealed that his bank account hadn't been credited with that month's pay. At night when he should have been eating and resting Shane was prowling around the hotel lobby fretting about his mortgage payments, his appetite, so vital to survival for a stage rider, eaten away by worry.

But still he carried on, trailing in a good 20 minutes behind the stage winner daily, sometimes with fellow sufferers for company but more often than not alone.

Riding into Bordeaux the previous day Steve Swart had beaten him in by barely two and a half minutes – the first really bad day for the New Zealander. Shane had little sympathy for his fellow Antipodean.

'It's all right for him – he's had one bad day, I've had one every day,' he pointed out.

'Never mind, Shane,' said Griffiths, 'some big guys will be suffering on those hills tomorrow.'

'Yeah, some little guys will be suffering, too – and I'm one of them,' said Shane. 'The question is, do I go eyeballs out up that first climb and then try and stay with them?'

'It will be different tomorrow – lots of small groups, you've got to stick with one of those,' advised Griffiths.

Shane, at least, wasn't the only worried man. Like Lenin in his sealed carriage the riders had been transported by special train from Bordeaux to the Franco-Spanish border town of Bayonne – a sort of Tour Express supplied with sleeping compartments and uniformed flunkeys dispensing the usual huge breakfasts.

The two-hour journey had given time not only to feast and sleep but also to look at the route profile and reflect on the trials ahead.

The map of Stage 13 from Bayonne to Pau in the Pyrenees showed three major climbs in the 141 miles, one of them the *hors*-category (steeper than first) ascent to the Col de Soudet. It was time for the climbers to lick their lips and relish the thought of handing out some punishment to the heavyweight sprinters, so dominant in the flat stages of the first ten days.

Like them, Shane knew that the time limits were more unforgiving in the mountains, with the climbers able to spreadeagle the field over a wider area and no slipstream deep in the pack to shelter inside.

While the riders click-clacked their way south from Bordeaux to Bayonne, the rest of the ANC personnel were driving the 120 miles to the rendezvous and muster point in the Place Général de Gaulle.

As the riders wheeled around the square before the start, the purple outlines of the foothills of the Pyrénées Atlantiques could be seen spread across the horizon like a waiting carnivore.

The views, however, were lost on Elliott, who was laying angrily into Snowling as we arrived.

'I wanted 22s on here,' said the team leader, indicating his gear sprocket. 'I asked you three times last night.'

'But, Malcolm, we didn't finish work until past midnight.'

'Well, you should have seen what time I finished washing and all that – 10 pm.'

'I'll tell you what, Malcolm, I'll go and see what everybody else is using.' Snowling returned within five minutes with the news that most other riders had their bikes in a bottom gear of 39x23 and Elliott wheeled off, half satisfied at least.

'It's all in Malcolm's mind,' said Snowling, 'he's just wasting valuable energy worrying about it.'

Timmis, as always, wasn't wasting anything. After listening impassively to the exchange, he pulled down his £50 sunshades and pedalled slowly away to register, back once again in his own private world, his mind attuned to the day's work.

It was a facet of his character that appealed to Woutters, the team director, when he met him. Ward saw Adrian's taciturnity and single-mindedness as professionalism, whereas Capper saw it as a fault. Capper couldn't reach Timmis at any level.

'It's his only problem,' said Capper of Timmis after a fruitless one-way exchange. 'I don't know what he's thinking half the time. I like someone who responds.' One thing Capper could not question about Timmis was his courage, as we were soon to see.

A struggling rider has one sure barometer of the trouble he is in. If he looks over his shoulder and sees the broom wagon he knows he is tail-end Charlie of the day, for the van and trailer that sweep up the fallen bring up the rear of the whole vast Tour convoy. Behind is nothing but road. At times like this the rider in trouble is like one of the characters in a vampire movie who has to get out of the forest before night falls and the shadows engulf him. With frozen fear in his eyes he rides desperately towards home and safety.

Shane didn't make it. Within 14 miles of the start he had dismounted and his first Tour de France was over. Sitting in relative comfort in the broom wagon, his bike stacked on the trailer, all the pressure was off. For the first time since his arrival from England he could relax.

Before the day was over Shane had plenty of company on a stage which forced 12 other competitors off their bikes and onto the plane, train or ambulance home. On the first-category climb to the Col Bagargui, through forests lined with French and Basque supporters, the pack splintered like shrapnel and some famous names and faces were quickly off the back.

Capper guided the ANC Peugeot delicately past Catch sprint leader Jean-Claude Colotti, his red jersey turned almost black by sweat. Just in front of Colotti some panting spectators were comically trying to push the giant Belgian Franck Hoste uphill. The veteran sprinter, winner of the green jersey for points classification in 1984, was oblivious to their struggles, his eyes glued firmly to his front wheel, perhaps dreaming of the day the race would land back on level ground and he could make someone else suffer. One of Hoste's allies, dressed like a bull runner in white cotton suit tied with a red sash, collapsed by the roadside exhausted by the effort of trying to run uphill with 13 stone of bike and rider. Others, dressed for the occasion in running shorts and vest, were in better training for the Tour. Clasping their list of competitors they singled out the Spanish-speakers for special favours, propelling them forward for 200 metres at a time, pouring water over their heads, or yelling '*Vamos, amigo*' into their ears from close range.

Capper was still officially driving the lead car for ANC, a decision which had upset Griffiths, the experienced rider and team director, but a pit stop by our leader had let Griffiths through to the front.

Capper, slowed by the riders left behind on the climb, was adrift of the action, but, close to the summit of the col, Radio Tour suddenly burst into life with a flood of information.

A Carrera rider had fallen and Timmis was one of the following pack who had crashed trying to avoid him. On the precipitous gravel-strewn descent the ANC rider had slid head first down the road, ripping the exposed flesh on arms and legs and tearing through the fragile protection of the Lycra shorts. The fall also bent his bike and Snowling had climbed out to give him a spare.

Timmis re-mounted without a word and set off in pursuit of the pack down the hairpins.

As we tore down the hillside behind the race the mountain looked like a battlefield.

A gaggle of photographers and white-clad medics marked the site of a spectacular fall by Hendrik Devos of the Hitachi team, who had taken off over the edge and was lying concussed on the steep grassy hillside. Riders who had lost touch with their service vehicles were stood by the roadside screaming for wheel changes as the heat of braking melted the glue on the rims and whole tyres slid off. It was complete bedlam.

Steve Taylor, who changed for one of the Del Tongo Italians, burned his hand on the rim of the damaged wheel, then lower down had his ears burned by a flatted and furious Guido Bontempi when he offered him a rear wheel instead of a front one.

On one particularly sharp corner Capper took his eye off the mirror and cut straight across the path of Jurco, the giant Czech, schussing down at high speed, and Jurco demonstrated his command of English with a string of profanities. Prudently, Capper wound his window up as he re-passed the irate giant: 'I don't want the bastard gobbing all over me,' he said.

Back on the level, Capper drove the car on at 90 kilometres per hour after the main part of the race.

Some 4 miles back in the broom wagon Shane had company as more and more riders abandoned.

'The Saronni brothers climbed in steaming,' said Shane in the Hôtel Campanile on the outskirts of Pau later when the whole crazy day was over. 'All they could say was "Madmen, madmen" over, and over.'

'We saw Hoste lower down,' said Capper, 'he wasn't saying much then.'

'No, but you should have heard him in the wagon,' said Shane. 'Jee-sus!'

Shane's demeanour had changed dramatically. He had his extrovert face back on, although his place in the peer group had subtly altered. He couldn't discuss the day's racing with the rest of the team and, while not a complete outcast, found himself gravitating slowly towards the mechanics and the rest of the staff.

While life went on for the rest of the ANC team, with another stage in the mountains the next day, Shane had only the journey back to Britain to look forward to – although he appeared to be experiencing difficulty in getting the fare from Capper.

'Have you got a crowbar, Shane?' asked Griffiths irreverently. 'Because you'll need it.'

Out of habit, Shane still ate what the rest were eating as his training had dictated for so long, but instead of mineral water he treated himself to a beer. The silent cloak that the others adopted in the company of 'civilians' slipped gratefully from Shane's shoulders. He was himself again.

That night the ANC squad had two new civilians in town. David Boon, one of the sponsors' management, had arrived with Malcolm Stevenson, the firm's PR man. Boon was like a hearty PE teacher, full of enthusiasm for the days ahead, working out where ANC would win their first stage. At dinner he became embroiled in an argument with a Dutch journalist we had befriended.

'You see, Elliott will win a stage yet,' said Boon.

'But, my friend, you need a team to win a stage,' said the Dutchman, his handlebar moustache twitching in amusement.

'Elliott will win in Paris,' insisted Boon.

'If he reaches Paris,' said the Dutchman. 'Tell me, are you with the team?'

'Well, I'm from ANC, yes,' said Boon.

'But what has the African National Congress got to do with bike racing?' laughed the journalist as he set off in search of Jan Raas and the Dutch Super Confex team.

Angus Fraser arrived late for dinner after tending Timmis's wounds.

'He looks like something out of a butcher's shop; what's more I think he's broken his thumb,' said the Scot.

Unused to the Angus exaggerations, the new arrivals showed their concern until he went on to relate the details of his latest fight and the day he'd almost died of asthma. Perhaps Adrian wasn't too badly hurt after all.

Next morning Angus was in overdrive, bawling at some of the French Système U riders for mimicking the hotel manager and regaling us with a story of how he'd hit someone – the wrong man as it turned out – for tying a can to his Peugeot estate after one of

119

the feeds. But for all his tall stories and afflictions, imagined or otherwise, Angus was trusted implicitly by the riders, probably more so than any other member of staff. Timmis confided in him constantly. And the big Scot gave a hint of the pressure he was under in his role as surrogate parent to the riders when he said: 'I'm their father confessor. The only trouble is I've no one to confess to. Who does the father confessor confess to?'

'Adrian's gone,' said Griffiths at breakfast.

'Where to?' I asked in alarm.

'No, I mean he's gone, knackered. You have to work a rider up to something like the Tour and Adrian is definitely the most delicate at the moment.'

'Does he know that?'

'He knows enough by now.'

Nevertheless, at the finish in Luz Ardiden that night Adrian was still there along with the four other ANC survivors after four more fierce climbs and 110 miles of racing. His arms and legs were scraped raw by the gravel and there was a red haematoma the size of a golf ball high on his thigh, so it seemed a somewhat harsh judgement to hear Boon, who had followed the day's stage from Pau up front with Capper, say: 'Adrian bottled out on the last descent today.'

Lourdes on Bastille Day was the night's stopover town, a sort of Blackpool of the religious world where the only miracle I could see was finding a place to park Boon's hired BMW, which I had driven over from Pau. A Norwegian from America's 7-Eleven team had won the stage and suddenly there were American accents everywhere, all telling each other in loud voices – but with no one really listening – how it was done.

One of them couldn't believe that the hotel would not accept his American Express card and was bellowing at the manageress: 'What kinda joint is this, anyway?'

Like Shane, who flew out that day, my role in the team had changed subtly, too. From deep initial suspicion I was now almost, if not quite, one of the boys . . . helping out with the French translations for Capper now that Fisher had returned to work in Paris, carting the luggage around and doing some of the driving.

On one stage I had felt a ridiculous sense of pride, of belonging, when Timmis with a call of 'Here' flung his sweat-sodden undershirt through the car window and hit me in the face. Not only was I part of the teamwork, but Adrian had spoken to me!

Unfortunately I also served as the impartial middle man in all the internecine warfare, a sort of go-between and message-passer for all the people who for one reason or another weren't talking to each other. At dinner in the Hôtel Adriatic in Lourdes, while the fireworks flashed and crackled outside to celebrate Bastille Day, I found myself squashed between the vast bulks of Capper and Fraser when the fish course arrived.

'Just what I fancied, a nice piece of cod,' said Capper with relish.

'This cod is turbot,' said Angus frostily.

'Cod.'

'Turbot.'

'I've been around harbours, I live in the Isle of Man, I know cod from turbot,' Capper told me without looking at Angus.

'My brother's got a boat and I've fished with him,' Angus whispered fiercely to me without a glance at Capper.

And so it went on to a background of thunderflashes outside, each man relaying their extensive knowledge of marine life, via me, to each other, until as if by divine intervention one last huge bang outside shook the hotel and ended the conversation.

After the humidity of Berlin, the fierce heat of the French flatland and the cold air of the mountains, next day's stage from Tarbes to Blagnac was to take the riders to another extreme.

With 35 miles left to the finish, huge black clouds heralded the approach of a thunderstorm and within minutes the heavens had opened and the roads were flooded.

As we passed Swart near the finish the water was almost up to his knees and he resembled a holidaymaker on a seaside 'pedalo', while the Peugeot left a huge sidewash like an ocean cruiser.

'It was ridiculous,' said Malcolm Elliott later. 'I thought we were going to ride and ride until we disappeared.'

In the confusion of the poor visibility and sweeping rain a break of three riders developed – one of them, Irishman Martin Earley, riding in spectacles – a break which Capper believed ANC should have followed.

Relations between the tour manager and his *directeur sportif* Griffiths had reached a non-speaking low over who was to drive which car but Capper's insistence that ANC should have chased what he described as 'that soft break' turned the air to frost. As Elliott passed Capper at dinner in Blagnac the team manager called the rider over. 'Watch it, Malc, he's going to ask you why you didn't chase that soft break today,' chortled Griffiths. Capper was furious.

'Only joking, only joking,' said Griffiths.

Then in a whispered aside across the table: 'The lads were pissing themselves when they heard him say that.'

Aloud to Capper: 'Tony, we just haven't got the team strength to chase down breaks like that.'

Capper glowered back: 'What time did the race start? Noon? Now it's nine at night, it's taken over eight hours to work that one out.'

At least they were talking again.

By now it had finally sunk in that travelling in one of the team cars was not the way to report the Tour. My French wasn't good enough to follow the pattern of the race on Radio Tour and as the second car always followed the last ANC rider we often found ourselves out of range anyway. Most journalists had their own cars and would follow the race until about 20 miles from the finish before accelerating ahead where by far the best overall view of the action could be had on the banks of TVs, thoughtfully supplied by the Tour direction, in the Salle de Presse. So, when Griffiths asked if I wanted to go ahead with Sabino in the Citroën to the hotel in Millau while the riders tackled the 145-mile Stage 16, I gratefully seized the opportunity of what I thought would be a leisurely drive through the French countryside away from the white-knuckle motoring of the team vehicles.

I didn't know my Sabino, the original boy racer.

By now Nick Rawling had arrived from England to take the place of Geoff Shergold, who had had to return to his work with British Gas in Southampton. Sabino wasn't prepared to wait for Nick, either. Within minutes of setting out from Blagnac he was doing 140 kilometres an hour trying to lose the Kas Mercedes van and its grinning driver behind. When he realised the Iveco hadn't managed to keep up he was amazed.

Sabino had evolved a canny routine for his hotel recce journeys, driving to that night's hotel as quickly as possible, unloading the cases into the right rooms, dining on the ANC bill and then relaxing. But the overnight stop in Millau didn't allow such luxury.

To Sabino's horror ANC's billet was an ancient college dormitory. The whole team plus the management, masseurs and journalist were in the same long corridor divided by hardboard partitions. Only Capper had managed a room to himself but even that was close to the huge communal wash area and its faulty dripping plumbing.

I could picture Elliott's face on arriving after another tough hilly stage and determined I wouldn't be around to witness his reaction. Even more so when the dining room was revealed to be a 300-yard uphill walk across the main road.

Fortunately the press centre wasn't far away and there, on television, we witnessed what even I recognised as the start of the Tour showdown.

The stage was won easily by Frenchman Régis Clère in a lone breakaway but behind him the gloves came off in earnest as the riders reached the last 6 miles of climb to the walled town of Millau where Roche, Delgado, Alcalá and Jean-François Bernard fought out a fierce uphill finish. In the crowded press room a low murmur of excitement, like the crowd reaction when a batsman plays and misses at Lord's, came out of the watching throng as one rider after another made what he believed was a decisive break but otherwise you could have heard a pin drop.

Back at the barracks we had, perhaps uncharitably, labelled Dachau, the silence there spoke volumes, too, as ANC arrived.

'I'm dreading Malcolm seeing this,' said Capper as we sat waiting for dinner in the school dining room with its wooden seats and plastic tops. Sure enough, Elliott soon stomped in clattering his table irons as he collected them and demanding querulously: 'Where am I supposed to sit?'

But his mood couldn't last and he was soon laughing at the reaction of the serving staff as Friedhelm mixed a huge bowl of muesli and yoghurt for the riders' breakfasts and then pretended it was his dinner.

One of the cook's relatives, an old man in his seventies, seated himself at the bottom of the riders' table and there was speculation about who their surprise dinner guest was.

Capper, sensing that Malcolm's mood was shifting in his favour, won another smile by guessing: 'The old bugger's won third prize in a competition and his reward is dinner with the ANC-Halfords Tour de France team.'

Perhaps Capper was right.

While his relatives lined the bottom of the table like spectators at a chimps' tea party, grandad happily tucked in with the riders, proud beyond belief that he was involved in the Tour de France. He had something now to tell his grandchildren.

In the dormitory that night my main concern was the possibility of snoring and keeping the team awake but I needn't have worried. As I drifted off I could hear the slap of flip-flops on the polished wooden floor echoing down the corridor.

'I'm not coming on this fucking little Tour again,' said Malcolm Elliott, to anyone left awake.

Stage 13: Bayonne to Pau, 219 kilometres, 34.585 kilometres an hour

Monday, July 13

Yellow jersey Martial Gayant had had his moment of glory and Système U were putting all their efforts into the cause of Charly Mottet, their logical choice of likely winner following the poor form of Laurent Fignon (perhaps not helped by his positive dope test just before the Tour began). Gayant in fact plummeted to 21st overall after this fearsome day of winding climbs and hair-raising descents, while Stephen Roche rose to third and Mottet took back the overall lead. The field burst apart on the first-category climb to the Col de Burdincurutcheta, sparked by a surge from 7-Eleven's promising young Mexican rider Raúl Alcalá, eager to hold on to the polka dot jersey of best climber. Alcalá got useful support from team mates Ron Kiefel and Dag-Otto Lauritzen before, on the descent that saw Adrian Timmis crash and Hendrik Devos ferried out by helicopter ambulance, Robert Forest of Fagor slalomed away on his own to head for the *hors*-category climb to the Col de Soudet at 80 miles. Alcalá continued at his own pace along with eventual stage winner Erik Breukink although by then Système U had begun the chase for Mottet. On the steepest part of the climb the Colombians Herrera and Wilches, tagged by Frenchman Jean-François Bernard and with Breukink in tow, zoomed ahead after Forest. The last big climb was the first-category Col de Marie-Blanque with 35 miles left and Forest, his big effort over, was caught and dropped. 'I tried to put in another effort on the Marie-Blanque,' said Forest, 'but after 3 or 4 kilometres they caught me. I tried to hang in but Herrera was going a bit too fast.'

The finish was down to four men – Bernard, Herrera, Wilches and Breukink. Breukink, the young Dutchman riding for Panasonic, had done little work all day, preferring to ride behind the wheels of others, so that when he attacked there was little response from his weary rivals and he went on to win by 6 seconds from Bernard, with Wilches and Herrera 11 and 13 seconds respectively in arrears.

Breukink was not considered a danger overall, but the stage had given valuable impetus to Bernard, Herrera and Wilches, who had gained 3 minutes 45 seconds on the other favourites.

1, Erik Breukink (NL) Panasonic, 6 hours, 19 mins, 56 secs.
2, Jean-François Bernard (FRA) Toshiba-Look, 6 secs behind.
3, Pablo Wilches (COL) Ryalco, at 11 secs.
4, Luis Herrera (COL) Café de Colombia, at 13 secs.
5, Eric Van Lancker (BEL) Panasonic, at 3 mins, 45 secs.
6, José Laguía (SPA) PDM, same time.
52, Adrian Timmis, at 14 mins, 40 secs.
80, Kvetoslav Palov, at 26 mins, 44 secs.
114, Guy Gallopin, at 30 mins, 37 secs.
139, Malcolm Elliott, at 33 mins, 35 secs.
149, Steve Swart, same time.
Shane Sutton, abandoned.

Yellow jersey: Charly Mottet.

Stage 14: Pau to Luz Ardiden, 166 kilometres, 31.672 kilometres an hour

Tuesday, July 14

Colombia's Luis Herrera is considered the best climber in the sport and untouchable in the mountains – if allowed to ride his own way. So his rivals do their best to ensure Herrera cannot ride his own way, by burning him off in the valleys between climbs or making sure that he is badly placed at the foot of climbs. The mountain-top finish at mist-enshrouded Luz Ardiden was a perfect case in point, with Herrera charging up the last 2 miles like an express escalator but too late to catch Norway's Dag-Otto Lauritzen of 7-Eleven who stayed 7 seconds ahead. The Colombian had mistimed it again for a stage win, although he moved handily up the general classification.

The day's action began on the return to the Col de Marie-Blanque where Forest had been passed the day before. Herrera was first over the top, only to be caught on the descent as the bunch regrouped. At the summit of the next col, the Aubisque, the Panasonic jerseys of Robert Millar and Teun Van Vliet were well to the fore along with Thierry Claveyrolat of RMO. It was Van Vliet who took off in a lone bid for stage honours with 20 miles left. Behind Van Vliet, Lauritzen, who had figured strongly on the stage into Pau the day before, left the chasing bunch in pursuit. At the foot of the last 3 miles of climb to the ski station Lauritzen was 2½ minutes adrift but Van Vliet had gone and the Norwegian steamed past his rocking, swaying figure halfway up. When Herrera, too, charged past shortly afterwards Van Vliet appeared to be going backwards and in fact finished almost 8 minutes later in a state of collapse.

In the meantime, favourites Stephen Roche and Charly Mottet were experiencing mixed fortunes. Roche was content to limit his climbing losses to Herrera and finished 10th at 1 minute, 36 seconds, but Mottet had had a hard afternoon, with Fignon having to pace him back when the yellow jersey lost touch 16 miles from the finish. Mottet finished almost 4 minutes adrift, although he had done enough to retain the overall lead.

1, Dag-Otto Lauritzen (NOR) 7-Eleven, 5 hours, 14 mins, 28 secs.

2, Luis Herrera (COL) Café de Colombia, 7 secs behind.

3, Andy Hampsten (US) 7-Eleven, at 53 secs.

4, Pablo Wilches (COL) Ryalco, at 59 secs.

5, Anselmo Fuerte (SPA) BH, at 1 min, 28 secs.

6, Pedro Delgado (SPA) PDM, at 1 min, 30 secs.

88, Adrian Timmis, at 15 mins, 15 secs.

97, Kvetoslav Palov, at 20 mins, 53 secs.

106, Malcolm Elliott, at 24 mins, 37 secs.

141, Guy Gallopin, same time.

152, Steve Swart, same time.

Yellow jersey: Charly Mottet.

Stage 15: Tarbes to Blagnac, 164 kilometres, 41.347 kilometres an hour

Wednesday, July 15

Stephen Roche experienced his first major setback of the Tour when an apocalyptical thunderstorm after 65 miles almost washed his dreams of ultimate victory away. After the skirmishes in the Pyrenees the leaders showed little appetite for a chase when Irishman Martin Earley and Frenchman Roland Le Clerc along with West Germany's Rolf Golz took off after the day's first Catch sprint at Lizos, barely 4 miles into the stage. With 30 miles left, the trio had a lead of 22 minutes but then the rains came down. Golz took the stage comfortably with Le Clerc second and Earley third, but the real drama was being played out behind them. After the village of Bragayrac at 74 miles, and with the roads awash, an attack from Système U – keen to win Mottet some time back – took the bunch by surprise. Roche for once was caught at the back and soon found himself 300 yards adrift in the second bunch, while a large group of 30, with the yellow jersey of Mottet prominent in the gloom, built up their lead. By the time Blagnac was reached and the downpour showed signs of abating Mottet and the front group were 1 minute, 7 seconds ahead and the Système U favourite had an overall lead of 2 minutes, 33 seconds on Roche.

1, Rolf Golz (WG) Super Confex, 3 hours, 57 mins, 59 secs.

2, Roland Le Clerc (FRA) Caja Rural, same time.

3, Martin Earley (IRE) Fagor, 4 secs behind.

4, Phil Anderson (AUS) Panasonic, at 11 mins, 47 secs.

5, Peter Stevenhaagen (NL) PDM, same time.

6, Gerrie Knetemann (NL) PDM, same time.

37, Guy Gallopin, at 12 mins 54 secs.

38, Adrian Timmis, same time.

47, Malcolm Elliott, same time.

74, Kvetoslav Palov, same time.

162, Steve Swart, at 19 mins, 27 secs.

Yellow jersey: Charly Mottet.

Stage 16: Blagnac to Millau, 216.5 kilometres, 36.249 kilometres an hour

Thursday, July 16

Former French champion Régis Clère, having been thwarted on one lone effort for a stage win (Épinal to Troyes), tried again and this time succeeded, although most of the media attention remained focused on the big boys behind. Clère went away after 15 miles and hung on for another 130, a colossal effort that left him exhausted on the stage's last 4 miles of twisting climb into Millau. Behind the Frenchman we saw some admirable exercise in team tactics. Adrie Van Der Poel of PDM set the pace for team leader Pedro Delgado, while Toshiba's Niki Ruttiman and Steve Bauer kept the tempo high for Jean-François Bernard. Dag-Otto Lauritzen and Ron Kiefel of 7-Eleven were performing similarly for Andy Hampsten and Raúl Alcalá, while Mottet also had his *domestiques* out in front. Finally, their job done, the team workhorses stepped aside and left the team leaders to slug it out on the final climb. Hampsten jumped away as if shot from a gun, but first

Delgado, then Mottet, Bernard and Alcalá responded immediately. This was a showdown indeed and when Delgado surged again Mottet was first to crack, losing over 1 minute – the time gained in the storm the day before – to Bernard and Roche over the final mile. With the finish line in sight, Alcalá sprinted away to take second place. Bernard, Roche, Hampsten and Delgado finished in that order behind the Mexican, who also claimed the polka dot jersey of leading climber.

Herrera, Alcalá's rival for climbing honours, had mistimed it all again. Midway through the climb he had shot away from the struggling bunch but his amazing ascent still left him 26 seconds behind the five big names in front who had punched and counter-punched each other to a standstill. Mottet retained his yellow jersey but had shown fallibility when the pace had changed on a major climb, something that Roche and the others were not slow to note.

1, Régis Clère (FRA) Teka, 5 hours, 58 mins, 21 secs.

2, Raúl Alcalá (MEX) 7-Eleven, 14 mins, 13 secs behind.

3, Jean-François Bernard (FRA) Toshiba-Look, at 14 mins, 14 secs.

4, Stephen Roche (IRE) Carrera, at 14 mins, 16 secs.

5, Andy Hampsten (US) 7-Eleven, at 14 mins, 18 secs.

6, Pedro Delgado (SPA) PDM, same time.

61, Malcolm Elliott, at 16 mins, 37 secs.

78, Adrian Timmis, at 16 mins, 53 secs.

91, Kvetoslav Palov, at 17 mins, 52 secs.

128, Guy Gallopin, at 19 mins, 26 secs.

158, Steve Swart, at 22 mins, 35 secs.

Yellow jersey: Charly Mottet.

CHAPTER 9

GOLDEN BOY

'PASS US ME HELMET, I feel aggressive today.'

Malcolm Elliott, despite the trial of 'Dachau', was having one of those rare and valued good days that an athlete learns to recognise and take advantage of and halfway through the Tour's 17th Stage from Millau to Avignon had dropped back to the car to collect his protective head gear.

'You watch, Malcolm will have a go today,' forecast Capper.

Capper, big boss or not, was almost touchingly eager to please Malcolm, the team's natural figurehead throughout the Tour. In Malcolm he saw the whole justification for coming to France, the man whose sprinting skills – and many good judges rated him the fastest man in the world when on song – would bring ANC their stage win.

Somehow, somewhere, Malcolm would be in the right place at the right time in the dive for the line and Bontempi, Van Poppel, Kelly and the rest would be blown away. ANC's Union Jack logo would be up there on TV on the podium at the end of the stage. That would shut the doubters up back home. That would delight the ANC management board – perhaps they'd even double their cycling budget for next year! Woutters, the original *directeur sportif*, had seen things differently. He had doubted Elliott's ability to reach Paris and labelled him a 'playboy', based on Malcolm's past reputation as a two-wheeled womaniser and for putting other things in life in front of cycling.

Most team managers and quite a few riders don't welcome wives or girlfriends on Tour. Sean Kelly once claimed that he remained celibate for up to a month before a major race, prompting one rider to observe: 'By my reckoning that makes Mrs Kelly still a virgin.'

Roche would rationalise: 'You don't take the wife to the factory, do you?'

Nevertheless, there were girls on Tour. Both 7-Eleven and Toshiba had female *soigneurs* – one of them engaged to the Panasonic star Phil Anderson. Urs Zimmermann of Roche's Carrera team regularly saw his girlfriend, Caroline, who was on Tour working as a journalist and, as one ANC rider related, Dane Jesper Skibby of Roland-Skala fell lucky when a girl turned up from Germany to see his room mate Didi Thurau. Thurau, who abandoned after the Blagnac–Millau stage, was not interested and Skibby did his best as an understudy. Elliott's attractive girlfriend, Julie, appeared from time to time during the Tour. Capper was far from overjoyed, although personally I thought she made a pleasant change at dinner amongst all the glum masculine faces . . . like a hungover male voice choir on its summer tour.

As it happened, Elliott three times came close to fulfilling the Capper expectations. At Troyes he finished 10th in the town in which he had spent two years as an amateur, at Bordeax, third after being baulked by a falling rider, and riding into Avignon he could have justifiably claimed – although Timmis and Gallopin tried their best – that only lack of support prevented him winning.

The day at Troyes perhaps illustrated more than most that this particular team leader was poles apart from the monastic and dedicated superstars like Roche and Kelly.

Elliott had two happy years in the town before he turned professional and there were several friends in the crowd cheering him on at the finish. While the rest of the team took off for shower, massage and food, Elliott was determined to look some of them up. When he finally climbed into the car alongside Griffiths, his eyes glassy with the race's effort and the strain of wearing contact lenses for eight hours in the heat and dust of the day, he found we had company.

'You go to hotel?' asked a little Italian who had been helping the Del Tongo team.

Griffiths reluctantly agreed, thinking (erroneously as it turned out) that Del Tongo were in the same hotel as ANC 30 kilometres out in Romilly-sur-Seine. The Italian sat there happily while Elliott and Griffiths made another call on another friend who ran a garage business.

By now I could picture someone like Kelly washed and massaged and with his feet up while ANC's team leader was still in his sweaty racing clothing driving around Troyes in the company of a journalist and an Italian stranger.

As we motored swiftly out towards Romilly our passenger spoke for the second time.

'You go wrong way.'

'What do you mean, wrong way?' asked Griffiths.

'I go to station hotel,' said the Italian. 'You go there, too.'

'No, Romilly, Romilly,' roared Griffiths, 'we go to Romilly.'

'No, my hotel in Troyes,' said the panicking passenger.

Griffiths exploded. 'You mean you wanted me to drive you 200 yards from the finish to your poxy hotel?'

'Throw him out here,' demanded Elliott. 'What a wanker!'

By now our friend was getting the picture.

'Madonna mia,' he waited clasping his hands together and rolling his eyes heavenward.

But as so often before Elliott could not maintain his bad temper for long and he persuaded Griffiths to take the anguished Italian back to town. After a U-turn across three lanes of traffic we returned to Troyes to drop off the perspiring and grateful hitch hiker.

'Nexta time . . . you walka,' said Elliott, in graphic farewell.

At Bordeaux after Kelly's crash Elliott came third behind Davis Phinney of America and Jean-Paul Van Poppel of Holland, although he had been forced off line by a crash in front and believed but for that he could have won. Coming into Avignon he had got away from the bunch in a group of four that included Phil Anderson and built up a 10-second lead. As news of Elliott's breakaway came over the Radio Tour, our Dutch journalist friend appeared alongside in his Audi Quattro.

'Elliott, eh?' he asked. 'But you see, Super Confex will chase.'

Sure enough, the Dutch team reeled in the break and a few minutes later the journalist was back.

'Van Poppel!' he shouted in triumph as he heard through his headphones that his big countryman had taken the finishing sprint.

Elliott had done well to hang on for sixth on one of his better days, although he had incurred the wrath of the Tour director for peeing close to some spectators.

Goddet, who had earlier described the Englishman as a 'handsome and amiable boy', shouted: 'You have done a disgusting thing,' as he registered the 80 francs fine.

At dinner in Avignon after his near miss I had been looking for a 'quote' for the paper and I asked a reluctant Elliott: 'Did Van Poppel go past you and the rest?' – meaning, did he come from behind or did he lead the sprint out?

Elliott replied with heavy sarcasm: 'Of course he came past, he finished first, didn't he?'

This was too much.

'Malcolm, it's no wonder people back home don't understand cycling. Nobody ever seems to explain to outsiders what's going on. That's why I keep asking such bloody stupid questions.'

Elliott must have taken the point because the upshot was that he agreed to an interview next day, the Tour's official rest day, to try to explain some of the intricacies of his chosen profession and about the dreaded time trial up Mont Ventoux which was to follow. Elliott took the rest day literally, sunbathing most of the afternoon on the hotel lawn with Griffiths snoring peacefully alongside in the next deckchair, but said he would meet me later for a beer in the hotel opposite.

America's 7-Eleven team were staying next door and the hotel barmaid had taken a shine to their team leader Andrew Hampsten . . . until Elliott walked in that is.

'*Qu'il est beau!*' she exclaimed. '*Très charmant.*'

Elliott smiled, probably used to this sort of reaction. While the barmaid twittered around the table like a little sparrow and in competition to the background noise of a busy hotel bar, Elliott talked fluently if a little wistfully about life as a professional cyclist.

I asked first about the Tour de France and its effect on him.

'Before the start of the race I knew one or two people who had ridden it before and you are told "You have to go out and you feel this and you feel that." But even the forewarning doesn't prepare you for what's to come, it's just the sheer duration of it.

'It's just so relentless. It has never really eased up, just occasionally you get an easy day. Even seasoned Tour riders kept saying how they couldn't believe it was such a hard race this time. So competitive. Because it was so wide open there was no clear-cut leader from the start and people were prepared to take a chance, take a risk. Even now I can't remember how I felt in the first week, it seems so long ago and I've gone through so many different feelings since then, feeling low then having morale on the stages to Avignon and Bordeaux. But on the day before I felt lowest.

'If you think it drags when you're in the car following the race, it drags that much more when you're riding.

'Even when you drift off to sleep and dream, all you do is dream about a bike race.'

Had Elliott performed up to his expectations?

'I think you always want more, always want to do better, and I feel I could have improved. If I sit and think about what I've done or what the team's done, it's reasonable. Particularly because we weren't supposed to be here until next year, it was rushed on a bit.

'But if I could rewind the finish at Bordeaux and play it all again I know I could win it.

'Yesterday [coming in to Avignon] I don't think I could have won, I just wasn't strong enough, but at Bordeaux I'd have followed Phinney when he came past me. If I'd have been just three or four riders up the line I might have avoided the crash, but it's all so hypothetical. It doesn't really change anything.

'In the mountains I haven't tried to burst myself because I know it won't make very much difference and I could waste reserves trying a bit too hard one day when I could try a little less and save a bit for the next day or the day after that. Then I may have to dig deep just to get inside the time limit. I think there's a lot of riders in the same position and now we know we've got to stick together.

'The hardest thing for me is the mental as well as physical. The first week was murder and I felt I was just going to fall to pieces and I couldn't envisage how I was going to get through the next few weeks. Two or three days were interminable with the heat and all the transfers and I just had to turn my brain off for a few days. It still seems a hell of a way to Paris, but viewing tomorrow on Ventoux as a bit of a rest day, just ride within myself and not try too hard, I think I can get through the Alps in the next four days. Then there's still a couple of opportunities left for a sprinter, into Dijon then into Paris, although that will be the hardest stage to win because everyone will be after winning that.

'If it's been hard for me it's been hard for others. A lot of riders are in the same boat. It's like a mental battle . . . you're hammering yourself all the time and when you're really in trouble your mind starts running through excuses, "That's not right, this is not right", and you can feel a bit of a pain coming on and it could get worse.

'But I couldn't stop, I couldn't make myself stop. People have faith in you and say you can do it so you have to go on.'

Was he surprised to lose three members so quickly?

'I was surprised at Paul Watson. I expected him to finish. Chesneau, I don't know what happened with Chesneau, but the first few days were such a joke and a lot of riders thought "What the hell am I doing here?" In circumstances like that it's very easy to think "I'm ill, there's something wrong with me" and get out.'

What about Ventoux?

'We'll just have to wait and see about that. The thought of it could be a bit demoralising. Say I went out there tomorrow and really tried as hard as I could and still got beaten by 10 minutes. I won't be going up so fast, I want to look after my brain cells for a bit.'

Doesn't it seem a hell of a way to make a living?

'It's hard on your body but it's healthy, and what would I be doing otherwise? I didn't leave school with any qualifications and they said I wasn't particularly gifted at school. I just used to have a good laugh, what you'd call a disruptive influence. I tried working for somebody when I was an apprentice after leaving but the routine of it was killing me, having to get up early every day and do the same thing.

'Some riders will retire at 29 or 30, maybe go on to 34, and they say that one of these Tours if you ride them hard takes a year off your life, but I don't know what I'm going to do when the time comes. Trying to think ten years ahead is a distraction, it could ruin your career.

'I still don't know if I could live over here in Europe. It's good money and everything and that's the bottom line, but I'd miss home in a lot of ways. When I've been away for a long time I look forward to getting down to the local with a few of my mates – you know, familiar faces you've not seen for so long. That's what I'm looking forward to after the race. It seems so long since I was last at home I've forgotten what the place is like, so much water under the bridge since then. There's always the feeling in pro cycling of not being based anywhere, you're always in transit. And you always have to look after yourself, make yourself eat the right things and that. Sometimes I have to force myself to eat even though I'm not hungry.'

Was he happy about the ANC organisation?

'Yeah, there's always a few loose ends and hiccups on the way, things could be tighter but I think when you get down to it and look at what we've done in the last two or three years it's amazing really. I think everyone will finish now, barring accidents or serious illness, although the next few days are going to be hard. They'll split into shreds in the next four days, the whole field will be in bits and pieces all over the Alps.'

What about the descents?

'I've never had a big fall – just little ones – usually you just spin off the side and it's just a broken collarbone if you're lucky when you're coming down descents like that and you pop a tyre. You're lucky if it happens on a straight bit and you can pull up. It's when you start trying to turn a slight corner at 40, 50, 60 miles an hour and you puncture then you're straight down.'

Before the interview began I'd told Elliott to reach over and switch off the tape recorder if he didn't want anything controversial on the record and the time was now approaching. I asked about the talk and the wheeler dealing in the *peloton* where cash can quite often ensure a stage win.

'A couple of times when we got away yesterday I spoke with Anderson, and had it lasted a bit longer I'd have said a bit more.'

What would he have said?

'I'd have said . . . aw, no, if it had gone to the end, I mean, I would have . . .'

Elliott reached over and clicked down the stop button on the machine. But by then I'd learned a lot more about cycling tactics and ethics. Capper and ANC would have had to have paid for Elliott's stage win at Avignon.

By now ANC's Tour de France was beginning to resemble a huge family outing. Fisher – Fish Face as Snowling had uncharitably christened him – had arrived back from Paris with his wife, a tiny, aggressive and faded blonde . . . and their poodle. There was also by now Mrs Capper, a large lady perspiring in her summer frock, and two teenage Capper sons, who immediately donned official team jerseys and expensive riders' sunshades.

Fisher's poodle was in a bad way, having been left in the family Rover in the heat in Avignon, and didn't survive the day, Nick Rawling burying it in the hotel garden. Two lively children scuttling around the hotel and sitting with the riders at meals didn't go down too well, especially with the usually unemotional Steve Swart and Elliot.

Capper's eldest son upset everyone when he christened Sabino 'Smurf'. Sabino may have had his faults but at least he was learning fast and was part of the team. Why, we'd even thrown him in the hotel swimming pool as a mark of proprietary affection the night before and even Capper had decided that he would employ the little Frenchman again if they ever came back to the Tour. The youngest Capper also fell foul of Griffiths when he announced that he would be following the next stage in the team director's car.

'Oh no, you're not,' spluttered Griffiths. 'You go with your dad if you go with anyone. I'm the team director and in charge of the cars and I say there's no more than three in a car. Boys shouldn't be allowed on this Tour.'

Fisher's Rover at least gave the team an extra option for the time trial up Ventoux, with a car needed to follow every rider as they set off at 3-minute intervals.

Mont Ventoux, a sun-bleached extinct volcano close to Carpentras on the outskirts of Avignon, had earned most of its notoriety when the English cyclist Tommy Simpson zig-zagged slowly to amphetamine-induced death on its slopes. The time trial 25 miles up from Carpentras into its thin air was regarded as one of the Tour's major ordeals.

Simpson's widow, Helen, had arrived with her second husband, Barry Hoban, and had been asked by Jacques Goddet to attend a remembrance ceremony at the monument in the hillside where her former husband had fallen 20 years earlier. The Hobans waited and waited but somehow Goddet had missed the appointment. When he finally arrived, after some fresh flowers had been laid by the roadside by the Hobans, the couple had to be persuaded to return and perform the ceremony again for the posse of photographers who had followed the Tour boss up the mountain. 'The Tour has done nothing,' said Mrs Hoban.

Carpentras and its narrow streets were chaos as a dozen officials with whistles endeavoured to sort the team cars into the correct file. I climbed into Fisher's Rover to follow Palov but there were problems in attaching the billboard with the Czech's name onto the front and when we set off the hardboard slipped down to settle in front of the radiator grille.

There must have been 400,000 people lining the roadside on the way up Ventoux, 400,000 half-naked fans who encouraged every single rider, coaxing, applauding, splashing them with water.

There was also plentiful encouragement from our non-cycling press officer.

'Dig in, Omar,' Fisher would shout from time to time, leaning out of the car window and brandishing a cigarette. 'Dig in!'

Palov dug in and indeed was going better than the Rover which, with its radiator covered, was soon overheating. I could picture the embarrassment if the car blew up before the rider but in the cooler air close to the summit the temperature gauge managed to stay just below the red area as Palov caught and passed his '3-minute man', Erich Maechler. For seven days earlier in the Tour the Swiss had held the yellow jersey of race leader but, like many other Tour *domestiques*, Maechler's greatest labours were about to begin.

Ahead lay Stage 19 and the first day in the Alps. Ventoux served merely as a lusty appetiser to the real thing.

Stage 17: Millau to Avignon, 239 kilometres, 37.963 kilometres an hour

Friday, July 17

For two days in the Pyrenees the Tour sprinters had struggled to survive, knowing their day would come again when the horizon flattened out and they could use their physical power on the big gears and their aggression in the bunched charges for the finish line. Jean-Paul Van Poppel, the 6-foot, 13-stone Hollander riding for the Super Confex team, suffered as much as anyone in the mountains but coming into Avignon he was ready to step back into the driving seat. By now the race was down to 165 survivors and teamwork was again to play a big part in the Dutchman's victory, although the action did not begin until the last 20 miles. Raúl Alcalá of 7-Eleven, seemingly untouched by his previous day's efforts on the Millau battlefield, chose the Pont de Nord on the outskirts of the city to make his attack, taking with him Adrian Timmis (trying to pave the ground for Malcolm Elliott), Allan Peiper of Panasonic and Jelle Nijdam of Super Confex. They were soon engulfed, but a counter-attack went out straight away from Phil Anderson, the other Panasonic Aussie, Marc Sergeant of Joker, Jose-Luis Navarro of BH and Elliott, who must have felt that his superior sprinting skills, along with perhaps an English-speaking alliance with Anderson, would give ANC their much-needed stage win. It was not to be. With 3 miles to go, the quartet were engulfed by the rolling tide of the *peloton* and as they crossed the Rhône the tactical jockeying began. Elliot got a good lead out from Timmis but it was Van Poppel and Bontempi, the high-speed heavyweights, who slugged it out over the last 20 metres, with the Dutchman getting the verdict by a foot.

1, Jean-Paul Van Poppel (NL) Super Confex, 6 hours, 17 mins, 44 secs.

2, Guido Bontempi (ITAL) Carrera, same time.

3, Manuel Jorge Domínguez (SPA) BH, same time.

4, Josef Lieckens (BEL) Joker, same time.

5, Teun Van Vliet (NL) Panasonic, same time.

6, Malcolm Elliott (GB) ANC, same time.

16, Adrian Timmis, same time.

22, Guy Gallopin, same time.

28, Kvetoslav Palov, same time.

159, Steve Swart, at 3 mins, 59 secs.

Yellow jersey: Charly Mottet.

Stage 18: Mont Ventoux time trial, 36.5 kilometres, 27.466 kilometres an hour

Sunday, July 19

Jean-François Bernard slaughtered the field on forbidding Mont Ventoux to take his first Tour yellow jersey – although surely not his last. With English-speaking riders threatening to take over their beloved Tour – America's Greg LeMond had won in 1986 – the French had been desperately seeking a successor to five-times winner and now retired Bernard Hinault. Jean-François Bernard, with his pain-racked ride to glory on Ventoux, filled the bill admirably, if only for a day. If Bernard's winning effort was a triumph of willpower and motivation it was also a triumph for advance planning. Bernard had brought some surprised comment when he was spotted warming up outside Carpentras on a low-profile time trials bike but there was method in this madness. The road out of Carpentras to the slopes of Ventoux rises gradually and Bernard and his *directeur sportif* Paul Koechli had reasoned that the Frenchman could gain valuable time here on the trials bike before switching to his lower-geared racing bike at the foot of the mountain. Close to Bedoin at 10 miles Bernard hopped off one bike, his team car drew up alongside and he climbed aboard his carbon-fibre road bike to tackle the winding 10 per cent slopes of the sporting rack known as Mont Ventoux. Bernard made a frightening picture as he rocked and rolled up the upper reaches, lined with crowds of 400,000 according to police estimates. With his jersey zipped down, his face scarlet with effort and mucus dribbling down his chin, Bernard looked like a man prepared to die for victory. He later admitted: 'I felt terrible' – and he looked it. Bernard caught his 3-minute man Andy Hampsten long before the summit and took another minute out of the American by the line. A similar fate overtook Scots climber Robert Millar, destroyed by Delgado on his way to third place. 'My *directeur sportif* gave me the split times for Millar on the way up because I thought he would be one of the best on Ventoux. When I passed him I made a greater effort because on stages like this you must finish "dead". Nevertheless, Bernard really surprised me,' said Delgado. Roche, who admitted making a mistake with his choice of gearing, was 2 minutes 19 seconds down on Bernard at the summit but still moved into second overall. 'I expected to lose a minute to someone like Herrera but I always believed Bernard would win,' he said.

1, Jean-François Bernard (FRA) Toshiba-Look, 1 hour, 19 mins, 44 secs.
2, Luis Herrera (COL) Café de Colombia, 1 min, 39 secs behind.
3, Pedro Delgado (SPA) PDM, at 1 min, 41 secs.
4, Fabio Parra (COL) Café de Colombia, at 2 mins, 4 secs.
5, Stephen Roche (IRE) Carrera, at 2 mins, 19 secs.
6, Martial Gayant (FRA) Système U, at 2 mins, 52 secs.
31, Adrian Timmis, at 6 mins, 57 secs.
38, Malcolm Elliott, at 7 mins, 41 secs.
105, Kvetoslav Palov, at 11 mins, 50 secs.
113, Steve Swart, at 12 mins 26 secs.
153, Guy Gallopin, at 16 mins, 50 secs.

Yellow jersey: Jean-François Bernard.

CHAPTER 10

FAR, FAR THE MOUNTAIN PEAK

IN THE 74-YEAR HISTORY OF the Tour de France the dizzy climbs and epic descents of the Alps have always been the traditional killing ground. The uphill finishes and 10 per cent gradients of the tarmac switchbacks of stages like l'Alpe d'Huez are the stuff of legend. Invariably the Alps are decisive and when Tour riders descend gratefully out of the clouds and head towards Paris the ultimate winner has usually emerged from a shattered and disintegrating pack.

It was Tour founder Henri Desgrange who decided in 1910 that the high cols of France would make an interesting variation to the flat and often tedious stages that had characterised the first seven Tours. But in those days most of the mountain roads were little more than dirt tracks, used for the transport of livestock by peasants from one valley to another. On the 1910 Tour most riders, without the sophisticated gearing of the modern racing bike, had to push their bikes over horrors like the 8,000-feet Tourmalet pass.

'Assassin,' one of them had shouted at the impassive and

unsympathetic Desgrange. Like his modern counterparts, the Tour de France founder believed that without suffering and danger the Tour would not be the Tour.

That philosophy certainly held good in 1987. The four days in the Alps would not disappoint.

By now 43 riders had abandoned but over the next four days the casualty rate was to almost double. Among the leaders it had boiled down to a straight fight between Roche, Pedro Delgado of Spain, and the French pair, Jean-François Bernard and Charly Mottet.

For the 164 racers left it was now a matter of survival. While the climbing experts like Herrera, the Colombian and Delgado floated almost effortlessly up and around the Alpine hairpins surrounded by the hysterical bawling fans and enclosed like boxers in a ring by the team cars and photographers' BMWs and Kawasakis, the less able would organise themselves into little struggling groups, partners in their dogged head-down perseverance.

At the first hint of a steepening the whole pack would break apart, with the climbers, the children in a sweet shop, rushing forward to play and the bigger men, the sprinters and the time triallists, thrown out the back like the discarded bags.

As the hills got higher the groups would get smaller until at the finish they would wobble over the line one by one, mouths to one side in an effort to suck oxygen out of the thin air, torn and bleeding from their falls on the descents and light-headed through hunger and thirst.

The 120-mile Stage 19 from Valreas, an ancient and tiny town in the Vaucluse, through the limestone rock-climbing playground of the Vercors to the ski resort of Villard-de-Lans saw Stephen Roche take the yellow jersey of race leader for the first time and Steven Swart of ANC out of the race.

* * *

Swart had been suffering for a week with pulled tendons beneath his right foot and the strains of pushing down on the pedals on five major climbs into Villard were to prove too much on a stage which produced almost unbridled aggression up front. While Timmis, Elliott, Palov and Gallopin, bunched together in a firm and fighting alliance 20 minutes adrift of the action at the head of the bunch, pushed and sweated their way inside the time limit, the blond New Zealander was forced off his bike. 'I just couldn't push any more,' said Swart later. 'I tried but when I stood on the pedals the pain was killing me.'

We had arrived in Villard, a modern resort perched on a shelf among the hills of Isère, to find Mrs Capper and Mrs Fisher helped by a bad-tempered receptionist looking after the room allocation at the horrific modern apartment complex that was to serve as the ANC billet. Phil Griffiths' girlfriend Judy had arrived from England, too, but Griffiths was keeping her well out of the way.

'They'll never accuse me of bringing outsiders into the camp,' he said with a pointed glance at the two women busy deciding who was sleeping where that night.

'There's no room for "civilians" in a racing team. What with them and the two brats it has really upset the lads. I've never seen Swart so upset and Malcolm's fuming. They are just not used to seeing outsiders at meals and things.'

Did he mean me, too?

'Of course I mean you. I've never known a situation where a journalist was allowed to travel with a cycling team.'

'But, Phil, you could have been lumbered with a real tabloid pig, you know like the characters who put mikes under beds.'

'Yeah, but if you had been a pig, you wouldn't have lasted the first two days. We'd have just bombed you out,' said the uncompromising team director.

Like Shane before him, the relief that the suffering was finally over was palpable and Swart came out of his introverted shell. The rider was due to leave at five the following morning and along with the three mechanics we had decided to stay up with him until dawn in a sort of impromptu farewell party.

After a few beers in the dining room we set off for the disco buried in the depths of the complex to discover drinks at £5 a piece, the first one being free on production of a ticket supplied by the burly doorman.

Swart, however, had a simple solution.

'Next time that guy has to go and answer the door I'll nip down and help myself to a few tickets,' said the New Zealander, who astonishingly seemed quite unaffected by all the alcohol.

Sure enough, the doorbell rang and Swart disappeared on his mission to return with a big grin . . . and a handful of tickets. When these ran out the rider helped himself to a bottle of tequila and we demolished it watched by its smiling, interested owner. Perhaps he considered it an honour to have his liquor purloined by a Tour de France rider.

'I've quit,' said Griffiths. 'I'm on my way. I've had it up to here with Capper. First of all he's been hogging the lead car and this business with his family has just finished me off. In fact the only thing that's stopping me setting off home now is that I haven't been paid.'

Griffiths was in the hotel doorway preparing for the stages from Villard to l'Alpe d'Huez and there had been a few hints, a few mutterings, that things were not quite right in the ANC camp. We'd heard from England that Capper's management company, Action Sports, was in financial trouble and that the bailiffs had been into the offices in Stoke to remove furniture and office equipment. The riders, while worrying about the next three huge Alpine stages, were also fretting about whether they would get paid for their month of suffering. So were the mechanics, and Steve Snowling, already suffering from the abuses of Swart's farewell bash the night before, was almost speechless with fury.

Mrs Capper had solved one of the problems, however. Upset because none of the riders were speaking to her she had returned home, Mrs Fisher close behind.

Stage 20 ran 135 brutal miles from Villard over the Col du Coq pass to the legendary uphill finish at the ski resort of l'Alpe d'Huez. The approach to the Alpe up 23 switchback turns was famous not just for the spectacle of the winding road and the surrounding High Alps but for its ability to break hearts and bodies.

There were close to 250,000 sunbathing fans patiently lining the mountainside, many of whom had camped overnight. I basked in the reflected fame and glory of the Tour de France, driving the ANC Citroën with its 'Officiel' insignia up through the clapping hordes and over the chalked exhortations to the favourites on the road and arriving in plenty of time to help unload the bags.

From the hotel it was a short walk uphill to the finish line, where I witnessed the deposed yellow jersey of Roche arrive – 5 minutes behind the stage winner Federico Echave of Spain and 1 minute 44 seconds behind the new race leader Delgado.

As always, the pushing pulling masses of pressmen and photographers were waiting as Roche, sweat-streaked and eyes glazed, rode slowly over the line, his head down resignedly as he disappeared in the crush.

Crammed with a dozen other journalists in the dope control caravan where Roche was waiting to give his sample, his thin legs propped on the bench and a bottle of mineral water in his hand, the Irishman looked like a little old man.

Unshaven, cadaverous and with his eyes unfocused by the day's efforts, Roche stoically and unsmilingly answered the same silly questions, as he had done on every other day of the Tour, until, finally, we left him alone and departed to convey his views to the world at large.

When he finally opened the door of the little caravan and stepped back out into the sunlight and the gaze of his public and fellow riders the transformation was startling. The smile was back, so was the twinkling confidence as he waved to the crowd. Like a film star, Roche plainly had an image to maintain.

The mask slipped a little later that night.

As the racing intensified and the Tour narrowed to a straight fight between two men, so too did the media focus, and in l'Alpe d'Huez Roche snapped for the first time under the overpowering pressure.

A group of British and Irish journalists, including Des Cahill of Radio Telefis Eireann, had gone over to his hotel after dinner and Des told me later what had happened.

'Roche really lost his temper,' said Cahill. 'He shouted: "All the French and Belgian journalists see me right after the race and then leave me alone. Why do you think you can call on me any time of the night?"

'One guy had flown out from England from one of the Sunday supplements and wanted a picture of Roche on his hotel bed wearing the yellow jersey but Roche refused and your man went away empty handed.'

Des, who formed a good relationship with Roche in the Tour of Italy, managed to get his interview, however, perhaps the strangest interview of his life.

Roche, to get away from the crowds of pressmen patrolling his hotel corridor, dragged his countryman into a broom cupboard where Roche spoke . . . in the pitch dark.

On the tape you could hear the rider's earnest efforts to describe the day's racing in between Cahill's spluttering laughter.

Stage 21 of the Tour. Day Three in the Alps. Another drive in the Citroën up an interminable Savoyard mountainside to La Plagne and the spot where three hours later Stephen Roche was to lie stricken and prostrate, oxygen mask over his face and his race seemingly lost.

La Plagne, another ski resort, is like a city in the sky, with a cable car serving the complex of apartments, where ANC were due to stay, from the main part of the purpose-built monstrosity. The stage included, figuratively speaking, the high points of the race at the 8,000-foot Col du Galibier followed by the 6,000-foot Col de la Madeleine and the similarly savage final climb to La Plagne itself.

Watching the last hour of the race in the Salle de Presse we had seen Fignon the Frenchman outmanoeuvre Fuerte the Spaniard and take the stage, and we had seen Delgado lower down, knowing that Roche held the trump card of the last time trial in Dijon in two days' time, distance his Irish rival only 1 mile into the last agonising 6 miles of climb. At one point the yellow jersey of the Spaniard held a minute and with just 2 miles to go, 45 seconds, surely Roche was cracked?

But then came the final thrilling, courageous – and ultimately ugly – drama. Roche would not allow himself to quit. Reaching, as he admitted later, deep into himself as he had never done before, he began his lone pursuit.

Rushing out into the cold sunlight to catch the climax, we watched Delgado wobbling slowly into the banner-lined finishing straight before, incredibly, the little figure in the red, white and blue Carerra vest appeared 20 yards behind weaving from one side to the other. As he lurched over the line the Irishman vanished under a wave of cameras, recorders and notebooks, all fighting, some punching, for the same 'exclusive'. Roche stretched a hand out for support but found nothing there and toppled on to the road, face turned to the sky and his blue eyes innocently vacant like those of a newly born child.

'Stephen, uncross your legs,' shouted his mechanic Valke as he fought with the hysterical crowd to reach the rider's side. The Vitascorbol doctor elbowed his way brusquely through with an oxygen mask and aluminium foil and Roche, breathing slowly and deeply, gradually came round.

Above him on the podium Pedro Delgado, the race leader by 29 seconds – later widened to 39 when the impassive Tour jury penalised Roche for feeding outside the permitted zone – was climbing into the yellow jersey.

After a short precautionary trip to hospital Roche returned to the Résidence Bellecôte to try and eat, sleep, recover and perhaps save his Tour. For the hunting pack of media, however, there was still a job to do. A group of French journalists tiptoed up to the sixth floor where Roche lay, in a bid to snatch a late-night 'quote' from the stricken rider. Knocking timidly on the door they were confronted by the minder, Schepers, who was about to dismiss them when Roche amazingly called out: 'Just give me half an hour.' Despite the traumas of the most dramatic day, Roche, the little professional, was still prepared to fulfil his 'duties'. 'I may not have won the Tour today,' said Roche, 'but at least I've made sure I haven't lost it.'

'Was Roche that stiff I saw being carried down in an ambulance?' It was 11 pm and another sponsor had arrived in the ANC-Halfords camp and was being wined and dined by Capper. Like many sponsors this one had developed the habit of saying the wrong thing at the wrong time.

Across the other side of the room, Delgado, despite the lateness of the hour, was still bright-eyed and buzzing, signing autographs, laughing with his friends in the PDM team. Perhaps like everybody else he believed the Tour was won and that 'the stiff in the ambulance' would never rise again.

By now the phone calls for Capper were increasing and the rumours and whispers becoming louder as the faces in the ANC team grew longer. Next day was the last in the mountains, with a 120-mile stage from La Plagne to Morzine. It was also the last day for Capper as he climbed into his transport and without a word to the riders drove out of their lives. 'I'll see you in Paris, Jeff. I've got to go back on business but I'll be there for the last-night dinner,' he had told me as we stood outside the apartment block.

Even I knew by then that we wouldn't see the team manager again.

Capper's departure, or more important the departure of the Citroën estate, left the team limited in its transport options and it was decided that I could drive the Iveco straight to the stage finish in Morzine. I wasn't exactly overjoyed at this news, as two days previously the brakes had failed as Nick Rawling drove the van through Grenoble and I faced a six-mile descent along dizzy precipices to the valley.

But with a muttered prayer and Des Cahill as a passenger I set out down the hairpins out of La Plagne.

Halfway down on the approach to a sweeping corner I put my foot on the brake and there was no answering pressure. With handbrakes pulled full on and to the accompaniment of screeching metal and helped by a large bank and convenient lay-by I wrestled the Iveco to a stop. Along with the riders' luggage and spare wheels and frames I was stranded, 100 miles from Morzine and our next hotel.

The Tour directors had decreed that the riders would ride down the hill from La Plagne to Aime, the stage start, and before long and preceded by scores of journalists in their cars, one of whom fortunately picked up Des, they came swishing down past the beached Iveco. Palov and Timmis glanced at the scene without emotion while Elliott called: 'What's up?' as he went by, but he had gone before I had time to answer.

Then came the *soigneurs* on the way to the feed, and a hugely grinning Friedhelm who, unable to contain his delight, chanted, football fashion, 'A-N-C, A-N-C, A-N-C', as he witnessed my plight. Finally came the team cars and Griffiths, who left Nick Rawling to cope with the logistics of repairs miles from anywhere.

I climbed in alongside Steve Snowling, who as well as mechanic was now performing as back-up driver. Like survivors from a shipwreck and with their captain lost somewhere at sea, ANC struggled bedraggedly on towards Paris.

Stage 22 from La Plagne to Morzine contained five more fierce climbs culminating in the bumpy ascent to La Joux Plane, the final summit of the 1987 Tour where Roche, who had recovered remarkably and was looking as strong again as anyone in the race, struck the body blow that was to win him the race.

Roche had Schepers, who dogged Delgado all the way up the climb, working for him and, although their skirmishes uphill were drawn, Roche launched himself down the fearsome descent in an effort to distance himself from the yellow jersey. Three years previously on the same descent the Spaniard had fallen and broken a collarbone and this psychological advantage, along with his fearless breakneck plunge, gave the Irishman an 18-second advantage by the finish in Morzine.

With his speciality time trial to come a day later in Dijon it was tempting to write that, with Delgado holding a fragile lead of only 21 seconds overall, it was all downhill now for Stephen Roche.

For ANC there was still some climbing left. Snowling had spent the stage into Morzine amusing himself trying to toss polythene bags full of water through the open sunroof of Griffiths' car in front and driving one-handed down the hair-raising descent from La Joux Plane but his good humour had gone by the time we arrived in Avoriaz, the hideous modern ski complex 8 miles above Morzine.

For staff and riders, morale was at its lowest and the tired end-of-term feeling was not helped by the muddy, rainswept sidewalks and boarded windows of a winter ski resort in summer. Whatever enjoyment there had been in the 1987 Tour de France had long gone by now. The team manager had deserted them and they weren't even sure if they were to be paid for their efforts of the last three weeks.

Tempers were fraying, too. Elliott complained about having to walk 300 yards from the apartment through the chill and downpour to the dining room, while Snowling and Taylor had to wash the bikes in the open. Griffiths exploded at a gang of young autograph hunters who pestered his riders at dinner. I rang the office to hear that Nick Faldo had won the British Open but no one in Avoriaz seemed interested. Indeed, some did not seem to know who Nick Faldo was.

England seemed a million miles away.

Stage 19: Valréas to Villard-de-Lans, 185 kilometres, 37.810 kilometres an hour

Monday, July 20

'It's up to me now to attack Bernard but I'm not telling you where or when,' said Stephen Roche as the Tour headed towards the High Alps. Fate was to hand him the chance high on the winding slopes of the Col de Tourniol at 63 miles. Again the stage was to turn not just on individual effort but on improvised teamwork. At 40 miles, with the Tourniol climb looming in the distance, a break of 17 riders developed, made up of many of the leaders' *domestiques* who would then be handily placed for pacing duties when the big names behind caught up. Roche had Eddy Schepers, Bernard had the Canadian Steve Bauer, Mottet was represented by Thierry Marie and Marc Madiot, and Delgado by Peter Stevenhaagen. Six minutes behind, in the main bunch, Roche decided to test Bernard's mettle. His surge brought a spirited response from the yellow jersey but close to the Tourniol summit Bernard punctured and lost ground. Racing etiquette normally dictates that you don't attack a rider who has punctured, so perhaps it was coincidence that when Bernard was within touching distance of the Roche-Mottet-Delgado group on a team mate's surrendered bike, Système U went on the offensive again. The attack came just as the riders slowed for the feed at Léoncel, the valley below the Tourniol pass, and although Bernard gave chase his chain came off almost immediately. It just wasn't his day.

The pursuit continued for another 30 miles over the Col de la Chau, down into the Vercors forest until, halfway up the first-category Côte de Chalimont, Delgado, tagged immediately by Roche, accelerated away. Bernard was now in desperate trouble, almost 4 minutes behind with no team mates to help him, and by the time Delgado outsprinted Roche up the final hill into Villard-de-Lans the Frenchman had lost his yellow jersey to the Irishman.

1, Pedro Delgado (SPA) PDM, 4 hours, 53 mins, 34 secs.

2, Stephen Roche (IRE) Carrera, 3 secs behind.

3, Marino Lejarreta (SPA) Caja Rural, at 31 secs.

4, Anselmo Fuerte (SPA) BH, same time.

5, Charly Mottet (FRA) Système U, same time.

6, Luis Herrera (COL) Café de Colombia, at 1 min, 6 secs.

100, Kvetoslav Palov, at 25 mins, 53 secs.

108, Guy Gallopin, same time.

117, Malcolm Elliott, same time.

139, Adrian Timmis, same time.

Steve Swart abandoned.

Yellow jersey: Stephen Roche.

Stage 20: Villard-de-Lans to l'Alpe d'Huez, 201 kilometres, 34.243 kilometres an hour

Tuesday, July 21

Bernard was down if not quite out and, in this no-holds-barred contest, Spain's Pedro Delgado was prepared to put the boot in. By now Roche had narrowed the threats to his ultimate victory down to the man from Segovia, and how right he was was proved on the hairpins of l'Alpe d'Huez. Over the sharp climbs and descents of the Chartreuse range, the leaders stuck together until the Côte de Laffrey, a noted Tour challenge, at 90 miles. It was here that Federico Echave of the Spanish BH team launched an attack, pursued by a group of six, with the leaders' 'heavy brigade' close behind. Echave arrived at Bourg d'Oisans with a 4-minute lead and the 8 miles of switchbacks up to the summit ahead but, behind, the chase had been taken up by his leader, Anselmo Fuerte, pursued by Herrera and Laurent Fignon, finally finding the form that once brought him two Tour victories. The Colombian took off up the mountain in an extended sprint while Delgado, too, had taken off to leave Roche and his yellow jersey straining behind. The Spaniard caught Herrera and with 3 miles left was the new overall leader on the road, although he faded later. Echave hung on to take the stage by 1 minute, 32 seconds, with his BH partner Fuerte second and Christophe Lavainne of France third. 'If they'd told me at breakfast I was going to finish third in this company I'd have laughed,' said the Système U *domestique*. 'I usually know my own limitations.' Delgado was the new yellow jersey – the first Spaniard ever – by 25 seconds. 'Not quite enough,' said Don Pedro.

1, Federico Echave (SPA) BH, 5 hours, 52 mins, 11 secs.
2, Anselmo Fuerte (SPA) BH, 1 min, 32 secs behind.
3, Christophe Lavainne (FRA) Système U, at 2 mins, 12 secs.
4, Martín Ramírez (COL) Café de Colombia, at 3 mins.
5, Luis Herrera (COL) Café de Columbia, at 3 mins, 19 secs.
6, Laurent Fignon (FRA) Système U, 3 mins, 25 secs.
75, Adrian Timmis, at 18 mins, 45 secs
76, Malcolm Elliot, same time.
124, Kvetoslav Palov, at 26 mins, 57 secs.
136, Guy Gallopin, at 31 mins, 49 secs.

Yellow jersey: Pedro Delgado.

Stage 21: Bourg-d'Oisans to La Plagne, 185.5 kilometres, 30.320 kilometres an hour

Wednesday, July 22

Cycle racing alliances are curious and complex affairs and nothing illustrates this more than the day that saw Roche and Delgado ride each other almost literally into the ground. Roche's game plan was to attack Delgado before the final looping climb to La Plagne, where he knew the Spanish climber held the advantage.

On the *hors*-category ascent to the 6,000-foot Col de la Madeleine he had 1½ minutes in hand on his rival. Roche's usual 'minder', Eddy Schepers, had for once failed his leader and Roche climbed the Madeleine in the company of Spaniard Pedro Muñoz of the Fagor team. Muñoz no doubt would have been delighted to see one of his countrymen win the Tour de France but by then every rider knew that Roche had signed for Fagor for the 1988 season and Muñoz had his priorities right as he helped his future team leader in his endeavour to put as much space between himself and Delgado as he could. The yellow jersey caught the lead group at the feed point at Aigueblanche where Fignon produced his favourite tactic of attacking through the feed zone hotly pursued by Fuerte, keen to make up for his near miss at l'Alpe d'Huez.

Within 7 miles the two riders – no threat to Roche and Delgado overall – had a lead of 3 minutes and the focus was back on the tussle between the Big Two. At Aime at the foot of the final climb to La Plagne Delgado spurted away to build up a 1-minute lead in 2 miles. Roche needed help to maintain his tempo and he got it from Luciano Loro of Del Tongo, an Italian prepared to help the leader of an Italian team. As the pylons of the ski station loomed ahead Delgado began to falter, but he obviously hadn't mastered the art of wheeler-dealing – when Spanish-speaking Fabio Parra of Café de Colombia caught him, Parra swept past without a word. By then Fignon, France's tarnished champion, had outfoxed Fuerte in the finishing sprint to win the day and leave centre stage to Roche and his incredible fightback.

1, Laurent Fignon (FRA) Système U, 6 hours, 7 mins, 5 secs.
2, Anselmo Fuerte (SPA) BH, same time.
3, Fabio Parra (COL) Café de Colombia, at 39 secs.
4, Pedro Delgado (SPA) PDM, at 57 secs.
5, Stephen Roche (IRE) Carrera, at 1 min, 1 sec.
6, Denis Roux (FRA) Z-Peugeot, at 1 min, 5 secs.
83, Guy Gallopin, at 34 mins, 15 secs.

93, Adrian Timmis, same time.

94, Malcolm Elliott, same time.

126, Kvetoslav Palov, same time.

Yellow jersey: Pedro Delgado.

Stage 22: La Plagne to Morzine, 186 kilometres, 29.855 kilometres an hour

Thursday, July 23

Schepers was not to fail Roche again. With two flat stages and Roche's speciality time trial to come this was Delgado's last chance to distance himself from his Irish rival, but he had two men on the fearsome ascent of La Joux Plane close to Morzine to fight. Or rather three men. Robert Millar – another new Fagor signing – paced Roche on the start of the climb, while Schepers marked Delgado all the way up, closing every time the Spaniard accelerated and generally getting on his nerves. Roche had made a formidable recovery from the fiery furnace of La Plagne and admitted later to feeling as good as at any time on the Tour. His two attacks on Delgado on the climb failed but on the downhill Roche took off with the faithful Schepers glued to his rear wheel and doing his best to get in the way of any Delgado pursuit. Within seconds Roche, taking every corner like a downhill skier, had stolen 500 yards and by the finish had taken 18 seconds back from his Spanish rival, a vital psychological blow. The stage was won by Eduardo Chozas of the Spanish Teka team, who had broken away after 46 miles and hung on ahead of Roche's downhill plummet to win by 43 seconds. The true worth of Schepers to Roche had been shown on the stage. 'I was stricken that I was not with Steven on La Plagne,' said the Belgian. 'I promised him I'd be there on the Joux Plane. I also told him that the efforts on La Plagne had taken more out of Delgado than Roche and that victory was there for the taking. I try and keep his morale high,' said Schepers.

1, Eduardo Chozas (SPA) Teka, 6 hours, 13 mins, 48 secs.
2, Stephen Roche (IRE) Carrera, 43 secs behind.
3, Pedro Delgado (SPA) PDM, at 1 min, 1 sec.
4, Marino Lejarreta (SPA) Caja Rural, at 1 min, 10 secs.
5, Jean-François Bernard (FRA) Toshiba-Look, at 1 min, 11 secs.
6, Fabio Parra (COL) Café de Colombia, same time.
98, Guy Gallopin, at 21 mins, 36 secs.
104, Malcolm Elliott, same time.
109, Kvetoslav Palov, same time.
110, Adrian Timmis, same time.

Yellow jersey: Pedro Delgado.

CHAPTER 11

AU REVOIR

BY THE TIME THE TOUR arrived in Dijon the Republic of Ireland had cottoned on to the fact that one of their most famous sons was about to win cycling's greatest prize. The ancient Burgundy city was awash with Tricolours and Irish accents.

Most had arrived without accommodation and a large group, including Oliver McQuaid, a member of a famous Irish cycling family, had solved that problem by drinking all night in the bar of the ANC hotel close to the railway station in Dijon.

We had worked out by now, based on the Saumur–Futuroscope stage, that over the 23 miles of the final time trial in Dijon Roche should beat Delgado by over 1 minute. As he trailed by only 21 seconds as the penultimate day approached, that would give him the race by about 40 seconds and the celebrations had started early.

The race had progressed from St Julien close to Lake Geneva, following a road transfer from Morzine, over the richest soil in the world through the vine fields of Burgundy to Dijon in an uneventful 142-mile stage.

* * *

Uneventful for the riders, that is. For Goddet and the Tour directors there was a minor industrial dispute to deal with. The 18 accredited photographers who followed the Tour had decided that too many restrictions were being placed upon them and downed tools in protest, riding line abreast ahead of the *peloton* and refusing to take pictures, serious indeed for a race that relies on sponsorship exposure for its life blood.

It was the last strike of the Tour, following a sit-down by ban the bombers close to Troyes, a protest by redundant steelworkers in the Pyrenees and a roadblock by shepherds on the Madeleine on the stage to La Plagne. Like many other sports with a high profile, the Tour de France served as the ideal vehicle for political and other demonstrations.

Roche and Delgado had spent the day watching each other like hawks and conserving their energies for Dijon. Officially, there was one stage to follow that, from Créteil on to the Champs-Elysées, but this has traditionally been the winner's victory parade, his lap of honour around Paris.

Roche for once in his life kept his door closed to the media that night in Dijon and, oblivious to the war whoops and rebel songs in the street below, had retired by nine o'clock. While his countrymen caroused outside, Roche prepared his body and mind. Tomorrow he would ride out of the gates of Dijon into history.

In the end Roche did beat his Spanish rival by 1 minute, 1 second for a 40-second lead, the same 40 seconds he could have lost in Berlin if the police had led his team, and not the BH team, up the wrong street in the time trial, and the same 40 seconds he had trailed Delgado on the final ascent to La Plagne before he took himself over the limit. Such are the fine lines between death and glory.

As ever, the meticulous Irishman spent the morning of a time trial in lengthy preparation, first riding over the course and then along with Valke carefully deciding on the gearing on his lightweight, low-profile bike.

Roche was due off at 3.37 with the yellow jersey of Delgado 3 minutes behind, a decided advantage for the Spaniard. Roche looked nervous as he stood astride his bike in the chamber leading onto the ramp.

'Good luck, Stephen, good luck,' called his swaying countrymen on the Boulevard Maréchal Joffre but Roche did not seem to hear.

Finally the gladiators were away and we sat back to listen to their progress on the Tour radio.

Fifty minutes later Roche was back to claim the yellow jersey for the last time.

There had been sterling performances from Malcolm Elliott, who had preserved enough in the Alps to finish 20th, 3 mins 53 seconds behind stage winner Jean-François Bernard, and from Adrian Timmis, 36th at 4 mins, 47 seconds, but every other rider in the Tour had suddenly become a bit player. Roche's wife Lydia and three-year-old son Nicolas appeared by his side, while over in Dublin Charlie Haughey, the Taoiseach, was making hasty plans for a flight to Paris to greet the conquering hero.

Buried under a scrimmage of photographers and journalists, Roche told us all there was still the last lap to Paris to come but he was just going through the motions.

Even Delgado knew that the race was over.

Next morning Stephen Roche took his last and longest walk of the Tour from the railway station at Créteil, 20 miles outside Paris, along the platform to the waiting team car. He walked alone deep in thought and perhaps savouring these last moments of privacy. Things for the Dublin milkman's son would never be the same again.

The transfer from Dijon had once again been aboard the Tour Express. There had been some wild speculation in one of the

French newspapers that the Spanish-speaking riders might gang up to thwart Roche but at breakfast on the train Elliott had voiced the mood of the *peloton*.

'If they do that, all the English-speakers and the French will gang up on THEM.'

Palov as always was deep in a book while Gallopin and Timmis had taken the chance offered by the 'wagons lits' to snatch another couple of hours' sleep. Roche himself was still fulfilling his obligation to the media, with a lengthy interview.

Six hours later and a few seconds behind stage winner Jeff Pierce, Roche and his yellow jersey crossed the finishing line on the Champs-Elysées, his arms raised high in the air in the cyclist's traditional salute and surrounded by a protective bodyguard of Carerra team mates and English-speakers, Elliott among them.

While the media fell on Roche, Elliott, Palov, Gallopin and Timmis climbed on top of the ANC team cars and rode slowly in a lap of honour along the Champs-Elysées, for the first time on the Tour all smiling at once.

'This is the greatest day of my life,' said Roche.

As expected, ANC team manager Tony Capper did not reappear for the celebration banquet, although his right-hand man Donald Fisher was there with his wife.

The four survivors listened impassively as Fisher said: 'Tony could not make it but he sends his congratulations.'

To which Palov the Czech replied: 'Congratulations, what for? We have done nothing.'

'But you have finished the greatest bike race in the world,' gushed Fisher.

'We have done nothing,' replied Palov.

Too tired to celebrate, the party broke up almost on the sweet course.

Griffiths rose to carry on his last duty as team director in France.

'Don't forget, Omar, Malcolm, Adrian, off at seven in the morning.'

'But will someone wake us up?' asked Omar.

The Tour may have been over but the habits of a professional cyclist were hard to break.

Stage 23: Saint-Julien-en-Genevois to Dijon, 224.5 kilometres, 33.560 kilometres an hour

Friday, July 24

The irrepressible Régis Clère took his second stage victory on what was for the main contenders almost a rest day as they prepared for the race of truth at Dijon. With 15 miles left, Clère broke with a group of 7 and took 3 minutes out of the dozing *peloton*, who showed little interest in a chase. Roche and Delgado spent the day deep in the pack watching each other like hawks and both finished with the same time in Dijon.

1, Régis Clère (FRA) Teka, 6 hours, 41 mins, 22 secs.
2, Jean-Claude Leclerq (FRA) Toshiba-Look, 3 secs behind.
3, Alfred Achermann (SWI) Kas, same time.
4, Gerrie Knetemann (NL) PDM, same time.
5, Henk Lubberding (NL) Panasonic, same time.
6, Eric Van Lancker (NL) Panasonic, same time.
14, Malcolm Elliott, at 2 mins, 56 secs.
37, Kvetoslav Palov, same time.
49, Guy Gallopin, same time.
99, Adrian Timmis, same time.

Stage 24: Dijon time trial, 38 kilometres, 47.221 kilometres an hour

Saturday, July 25

And so the day of reckoning dawned. With the nearest rival, Bernard, 4 minutes adrift overall, the final time trial was a two-horse race. Course inspection in the morning revealed a stage suited to Roche, with only one third-category climb and a short ascent near the finish to tip the balance in Delgado's favour. Roche had reasoned correctly that most gains would come in the flatter first 15 miles, and after 6 miles he was 46 seconds up on his rival and the new race leader on the road. Delgado came back on the stage's two climbs but by the finish was 1 minute, 1 second behind and Roche was the yellow jersey – by 40 seconds – for the last time.

Alongside the Irishman on the victory podium was stage winner Jean-François Bernard, who had clocked the day's fastest time of 48 minutes, 17 seconds.

1, Jean-François Bernard (FRA) Toshiba-Look, 48 mins, 17 secs.
2, Stephen Roche (IRE) Carrera, 1 min, 44 secs behind.
3, Marino Lejarreta (SPA) Caja-Rural, at 2 mins, 28 secs.
4, Jesper Skibby (DAN) Roland-Skala, at 2 mins, 30 secs.
5, Raúl Alcalá (MEX) 7-Eleven, at 2 mins, 33 secs.
6, Miguel Indurain (SPA) Reynolds-Seur, at 2 mins, 35 secs.
20, Malcolm Elliott, at 3 mins, 53 secs.
36, Adrian Timmis, at 4 mins, 47 secs.
52, Guy Gallopin, at 5 mins, 34 secs.
58, Kvetoslav Palov, at 5 mins, 46 secs.

Stage 25: Créteil to Paris, 192 kilometres, 38.731 kilometres an hour

Sunday, July 26

Everyone wants to win the last stage in Paris – none more so than the French – so it was a surprise to see only two in the first 15 when Roche's victory lap of honour around the Champs-Elysées was over. After a leisurely start out of Créteil, the riders warmed to their task on the closing 25 miles and six laps up and down the famous Paris avenue. After some early offence from Régis Clère (who else?) and some half-hearted and unsuccessful sorties from the *peloton*, an eight-man break developed promisingly. With half a mile left the group was being reeled in as the bunch speeded up, all keen to take the ultimate accolade of victory in Paris, but America's Jeff Pierce had saved something and his final attack went unchallenged. An American in Paris, indeed!

While Roche was feted by the French president and Charlie Haughey, the Taoiseach, Delgado accepted his defeat with good grace. 'It's not so terrible for me to lose the Tour,' said the Spaniard. 'I knew Stephen was so much better in the time trial and he had one big thing in his favour I believe – in the last week there was very little heat and that would have favoured me. I'm a bit sad today. I got up this morning and instead of the yellow jersey put on my usual PDM jersey. It's very nice, you know, to put on the yellow jersey in the morning . . .'

1, Jeff Pierce (US) 7-Eleven, 4 hours, 57 mins, 26 secs.

2, Steve Bauer (CAN) Toshiba-Look, 1 sec behind.

3, Wim Van Eynde (BEL) Joker, at 5 secs.

4, Peter Stevenhaagen (NL) PDM, at 7 secs.

5, Adrie Van Der Poel (NL) PDM, at 11 secs.

6, Acacio Da Silva (POR) Kas, same time.

22, Malcolm Elliott, at 17 secs.

26, Guy Gallopin, same time.

59, Adrian Timmis, same time.

80, Kvetoslav Palov, same time.

Overall

1, Stephen Roche (IRE) Carrera, 115 hours, 27 mins, 42 secs (4,231 kilometres at 36.645 kilometres an hour).

2, Pedro Delgado (SPA) PDM, 40 secs behind.

3, Jean-François Bernard (FRA) Toshiba-Look, at 2 mins, 13 secs.

4, Charly Mottet (FRA) Système U, at 6 mins, 40 secs.

5, Luis Herrera (COL) Café de Colombia, at 9 mins, 32 secs.

6, Fabio Parra (COL) Café de Colombia, at 16 mins, 53 secs.

7, Laurent Fignon (FRA) Système U, at 18 mins, 24 secs.

8, Anselmo Fuerte (SPA) BH, at 18 mins, 33 secs.

9, Raúl Alcalá (MEX) 7-Eleven, at 21 mins, 49 secs.

10, Marino Lejarreta (SPA) Caja-Rural, at 26 mins, 13 secs.

70, Adrian Timmis (GB) ANC-Halfords, at 2 hours, 19 mins, 21 secs.

94, Malcolm Elliott (GB) ANC-Halfords, at 2 hours, 48 mins, 39 secs.

103, Kvetoslav Palov (CZE) ANC-Halfords, at 2 hours, 59 mins, 4 secs.

133, Guy Gallopin (FRA) ANC-Halfords, at 3 hours, 49 mins, 48 secs.

Started: 207.
Finished: 135.

CHAPTER 12

THE NEXT HORIZON

HAVING CONQUERED FIRST ITALY AND then France, **Stephen Roche** could now think about conquering the world. Only one rider before had ever won the Tour of Italy, the Tour de France and the World Championships in the same season and that was the greatest of them all, the Belgian 'Cannibal' Eddy Merckx.

As in the days before the Tour de France, Roche was uncertain about his chances. His preparations were as low key as ever, helped by the thought that the Villach course in Austria, venue for the World's, was designed for the sprinter not an all-rounder. Tired and without any motivation Roche rode a few criteriums, the carefully choreographed European town road races which are the traditional lucrative earners for post-Tour riders, but could not find the urge to get into a serious training routine. He had already decided that he would ride for his countryman Sean Kelly at Villach, and along with Irish team mates Paul Kimmage and Martin Earley began to prepare, feeling gradual improvement as Villach grew closer.

When the Irish team rode up to the start line in a downpour they still believed that if all went to plan this would be Kelly's race. With 2 miles left their strategy was looking good – Kelly and Roche were in the leading group after six and a half hours of racing around the rain-sodden Austrian circuit – but when Roche went away in a group of five with 1 mile left the Dubliner looked round for his countryman to find him dropped. It was now up to him, and putting his head down Roche went away, amazingly outsprinting the sprinters and crossing the line with a 20-yard lead. Now for 1988 he would wear the rainbow jersey of world champion. Roche had joined Merckx at the highest pinnacle of the sport and could name his price for the season.

During the Tour de France much of Roche's spare time had been taken, when he was not talking to the press, in negotiations with the Spanish-sponsored, French-based team Fagor. Like every rider whose rise or fall in the professional ranks depended on Tour performance, Roche was looking around. After the Tour of Italy Roche's days with Carrera were clearly numbered and the £400,000 a year contract offered by Fagor suited him nicely . . . as long as Valke and Schepers went with him, plus a few others who had helped or impressed the Irishman throughout the year. Like five-times Tour de France winner Bernard Hinault before him, Roche's stature guaranteed that he could pick and choose his cohorts.

Malcolm Elliott, formerly of ANC-Halfords, was the Roche/ Fagor choice as team sprinter and Elliott was to ride alongside the Irishman in the red and white jersey of Fagor in the following year's Tour de France at a reputed salary of £45,000 a year. Despite his doubts about living abroad, expressed to me in Avignon, Elliott had taken the plunge – although he was still hoping to find a place guesting for a British team in the 1988 Milk Race. Wisely, he didn't want to be forgotten at home.

Adrian Timmis, along with another British rider Joey McLoughlin, also had little difficulty in finding a higher rung on the cycling ladder. He signed for the French Z-Peugeot team, riding for the same *directeur sportif* who had done door-to-door battle with Capper and his ANC team car on the 17th Stage from Millau to Avignon.

Paul Watson, despite his flop on the stage from Strasbourg to Épinal, had still impressed enough to earn a contract with the Belgium team Hitachi.

Steve Swart returned to his native New Zealand and **Kvetoslav Palov**, the Czech defector who finished the Tour so strongly, to his adopted country of Australia – before both signed, along with **Bernard Chesneau**, for a new team, CEFB, run by none other than **Ward Woutters**.

Shane Sutton and **Graham Jones** would both race in the United Kingdom again – Sutton for Interent-Dawes and Jones as captain of Emmelle-MBK.

Guy Gallopin, the Frenchman, retired from competitive cycling to act as assistant *directeur sportif* to Système U.

Of the mechanics, **Steve Snowling** worked full-time on the Continent the following season, while **Steve Taylor** and **Nick Rawling** returned to their full-time jobs as assistants in bicycle shops. **Geoff Shergold** continued to work for British Gas in Southampton.

Head *soigneur* **Angus Fraser** returned to Meadowbank Stadium to tend the pulls and strains of injured sportsmen and women. **Friedhelm Steinborn**, **Roger Van Der Vloet** and **Sabino Pignatelli** had little difficulty in finding work in Continental cycling teams.

Ward Woutters continued to work for the Belgian Water Board, between *directeur sportif* duties.

As for **Tony Capper**, the man who like Frankenstein created and then destroyed the ANC-Halfords cycling team, he continued to live as a tax exile in the Isle of Man. Within a month of the end of the Tour he had withdrawn his interest in the team's management company, Action Sports. His two fellow directors wound the company up, leaving Griffiths, Mick Morrison (who helped run the office in Stoke on Trent) and two secretaries without a job. In February 1988, the first creditors' meeting was held and Capper arrived with claim for £50,000.

At the time this book was first published, the nine riders still hadn't been paid for the month spent on the Tour de France.

WHO WON WHAT

TOTAL PRIZE MONEY IN THE Tour amounted to about £630,000 split into 21 different categories.

The main winners were:

Overall winner (yellow jersey): Stephen Roche (Ireland), £18,000 and a holiday flat in the Pyrenees worth £12,000. Plus a Peugeot 405 SR Injection worth £11,500.

Points classification for the number of highest finishes (green jersey): Jean Paul Van Poppel (Holland), £3,200.

Best climber (polka dot jersey): Luis Herrera (Colombia): £1,800.

Best young rider under-24 (white jersey): Raúl Alcalá (Mexico), £1,500.

Intermediate 'Catch' sprints (red jersey): Gilbert Duclos-Lasalle (France), £1,000.

Performance classification (multi-coloured jersey): Jean-François Bernard (France), £2,000.

Best time triallist: Jean-François Bernard, £1,800.

Overall team winners: Système U (France), £4,000.

Overall team points winners: Système U, £1,300.

Each stage winner won a cash prize of £1,800, a diamond-studded map of France worth £2,000, plus a Peugeot Junior car worth £4,500.

French bank Crédit Lyonnais gave an extra £5,000 to the overall winner and £3,000 to the best young rider.

In addition there were:

A prize of £1,500, the Henri Desgrange Prize, for the first rider across the Col du Galibier on Stage 21.

A prize of £1,000, the Charles de Gaulle prize, for the first rider to reach de Gaulle's birthplace at Colombey-les-deux-Églises on Stage 7.

Prizes of £150 for sprint winner on the Champs-Elysées on Stage 25.

A prize of £350 for the rider voted the most affable on the Tour by his fellow riders.

A prize of £800 for the rider considered the most combative.

WHO LOST WHAT

THE *COMMISSAIRES* WHO FOLLOWED THE Tour handed out fines, after consultation with the race jury, on a daily basis. The most numerous, along with typical penalties, were:

Dangerous driving by a *directeur sportif*: £75.
Pushing a rider: £11 for the rider and £80 for the *directeur sportif*.
Pacing a rider with the team car: £19 for the rider and £80 for the *directeur sportif*.
Opening a team car door on the left: £37.
Not displaying a competitor's number: £19.
Not signing on before a stage: £11.
Having two team cars in the first rank of the race convoy: £10.
Throwing rubbish out of the car window close to the *peloton*: £10.
Feeding from the team car in the *peloton*: £10.

Three riders – Guido Bontempi, Dietrich Thurau and Silvano Contini – were found guilty of doping. As first offenders, they were each fined £500, incurred a 10-minute time penalty, placed last in the relevant stage and given a one-month suspended ban from the sport.

The *directeur sportif* of Système U, Cyrille Guimard, was thrown out of Stage 23 because his team descended from La Plagne in their vehicles instead of on their bikes as requested by the Tour Direction.

WHO WAS WHO

A TOTAL OF 23 TEAMS and 207 riders from 22 different nations began the Tour de France 1987. After 25 stages and 2,629 miles, 135 finally arrived in Paris. In terms of survival rate the most sucessful teams were Système U of France and Café de Colombia of South America, which both finished with their full complement of nine. The least successful were the Italian Supermercati and the Colombian Ryalco squads, which finished with just two riders each.

The Tour line-ups were:

TOSHIBA-LOOK-LA VIE CLAIRE (France)

Sponsors: Electrical goods manufacturers, ski and cycle goods

Directeur sportif: Paul Koechli

1, Jean-François Bernard

2, Kim Andersen

3, Steve Bauer

4, Charles Berard

5, Dominique Garde

*6, Heinz Imboden

7, Jean-Claude Leclerq

*8, Niki Ruttiman

9, Guido Winterberg

CARRERA JEANS (Italy)

Sponsors: Jeans manufacturers and kitchenware

Directeur sportif: David Boifava

11, Stephen Roche

12, Guido Bontempi

13, Davide Cassani

14, Massimo Ghirotto

15, Erich Maechler

16, Jorgen Pedersen

17, Giancarlo Perini

18, Eddy Schepers

*19, Urs Zimmermann

HITACHI-MARC-ROSSIN (Belgium)

Sponsors: Electrical goods and bicycle makers

Directeur sportif: Albert De Kimpe

21, Claude Criquielion

*22, Hendrik Devos

23, Rudy Dhaehens

24, Fabian Fuchs

25, Jos Haex

*26, Jos Jacobs

27, Stefan Morjean

* Abandoned

28, Jean-Philippe Van Den Brande
29, Jan Wijnants

Z-PEUGEOT (France)

Sponsors: Bicycle manufacturers
Directeur sportif: Roger Legeay
31, Pascal Simon
32, Frédéric Brun
33, Bruno Cornillet
34, Gilbert Duclos-Lasalle
35, Jean-Louis Gauthier
*36, Gilbert Glaus
37, Denis Roux
38, Jerome Simon
*39, Bruno Wojtinek

BH (Spain)

Sponsors: Bicycle manufacturers
Directeur sportif: Javier Mínguez
41, Anselmo Fuerte
42, Francisco Antequera
43, Philippe Bouvatier
*44, Laudelino Cubino
45, Manuel Jorge Domínguez
46, Federico Echave
47, José Luis Navarro
*48, Francisco Rodríguez
49, Guido Van Calster

* Abandoned

PDM (The Netherlands)

Sponsors: Video tape manufacturers
Directeur sportif: Jan Gisbers
51, Pedro Delgado
52, Gerrie Knetemann
53, José Laguia
54, Jorg Müller
*55, Stefan Mutter
*56, Steven Rooks
57, Peter Stevenhaagen
58, Gert-Jan Theunisse
59, Adrie Van Der Poel

SYSTÈME U (France)

Sponsors: Supermarket chain
Directeur sportif: Cyrille Guimard
61, Laurent Fignon
62, Bernard Gavillet
63, Martial Gayant
64, Christophe Lavainne
65, Marc Madiot
66, Yvon Madoit
67, Thierry Marie
68, Charly Mottet
69, Pascal Poisson

REYNOLDS-SEUR-SADA (Spain)

Sponsors: Aluminium foil makers
Directeur sportif: José Miguel Echavarri
*71, Ángel Arroyo

* Abandoned

*72, Dominique Arnaud

73, Samuel Cabrera

74, Marc Gomez

75, Julian Gorospe

*76, Ruben Gorospe

77, J. Hernández Úbeda

78, Miguel Indurain

*79, Ángel Ocana

TEKA (Spain)

Sponsors: Domestic appliance manufacturer

Directeur sportif: José Antonio González Linares

81, Raimund Dietzen

82, Enrique Aja

*83, Jesús Blanco

84, Eduardo Chozas

85, Régis Clère

86, Alfonso Gutiérrez

87, Carlos Hernández

88, Peter Hilse

89, Jesús Rodríguez

RYALCO-MANZANA-POSTOBON (Colombia)

Sponsors: Soft drinks makers

Directeur sportif: Raul Meza

*91, Pablo Wilches

*92, Alberto Camarco

*93, Arsenio Chaparro

94, Omar Hernández

*95, Carlos Jaramillo

*96, Gerardo Moncada

* Abandoned

97, Nestor Mora
*98, Pedro-Saul Morales
*99, Oscar Vargas

RMO-MERAL-MAVIC (France)

Sponsors: Employment agency and bike manufacturers
Directeur sportif: Bernard Thevenet
*101, Patrick Esnault
102, André Chappuis
*103, Thierry Claveyrolat
*104, Jean-Claude Colotti
*105, Paul Kimmage
106, Gilles Mas
107, Jean-François Rault
108, Bernard Vallet
*109, Michel Vermote

CAJA-RURAL-ORBEA (Spain)

Sponsors: Bike manufacturers
Directeur sportif: Domingo Perurena
111, Marino Lejarreta
112, Roque de la Cruz
113, Mathieu Hermans
114, Pascal Jules
115, Roland Le Clerc
116, Joaquim Mujika
*117, Erwin Nijboer
*118, Pello-Ruiz Cabestany
119, José Salvador Sanchis

* Abandoned

FAGOR (France)

Sponsors: Domestic appliance manufacturers
Directeur sportif: Pierre Bazo
121, Pedro Muñoz
122, Jean Claude Bagôt
123, Jean-René Bernaudeau
124, Eric Caritoux
125, Martin Earley
126, Robert Forest
127, Franck Hoste
128, François LeMarchand
*129, Sean Yates

CAFÉ DE COLOMBIA (Colombia)

Sponsors: Coffee manufacturers
Directeur sportif: Rafael Niño
131, Luis Herrera
132, Rafael Acevedo
133, Argemiro Bohorquez
134, Julio-César Cadena
135, Juan-Carlos Castillo
136, Marco-Antonio León
137, Fabio Parra
138, Cristóbal Pérez
139, Martín Ramírez

SUPER CONFEX-KWANTUM-YOKO (The Netherlands)

Sponsors: Supermarket chain
Directeur sportif: Jan Raas

* Abandoned

141, Maarten Ducrot

142, Rolf Golz

*143, Gert Jakobs

144, Jelle Nijdam

145, Ludo Peeters

146, Luc Roosen

147, Gerrie Solleveld

148, Jean-Paul Van Poppel

*149, Nico Verhoeven

PANASONIC-ISOSTAR (The Netherlands)

Sponsors: Electrical goods and energy drinks

Directeur sportif: Peter Post

151, Phil Anderson

152, Erik Breukink

153, Theo De Rooy

154, Henk Lubberding

155, Robert Millar

156, Guy Nulens

*157, Allan Peiper

158, Eric Van Lancker

159, Teun Van Vliet

DEL TONGO-COLNAGO (Italy)

Sponsors: Furniture makers

Directeur sportif: Pietro Algeri

*161, Guiseppe Saronni

162, Silvano Contini

*163, Czeslaw Lang

164, Luciano Loro

* Abandoned

*165, Lech Piasecki
166, Maurizio Piovani
167, Allessandro Pozzi
*168, Alberto Saronni
*169, Ennio Vanotti

KAS-MIKO-MAVIC (Spain)

Sponsors: Soft drinks firm
Directeur sportif: Christian Rumeau
*171, Sean Kelly
172, Alfred Achermann
173, Acacio da Silva
*174, Inaki Gaston
*175, Stephan Joho
*176, Luis Javier Lukin
*177, Javier Murguialday
178, Celestino Prieto
179, Gilles Sanders

JOKER-EMERXIL-EDDY MERCKX (Belgium)

Sponsors: Lottery and bike manufacturer
Directeur sportif: Walter Godefroot
*181, Marc Sergeant
182, Beat Breu
183, Michel Dernies
184, Jan Goesens
185, Josef Lieckens
*186, Jan Nevens
*187, Peter Roes
*188, Franck Van De Vyver

* Abandoned

189, Wim Van Eynde

7-ELEVEN-HOONVED (United States)
Sponsors: Store chain and domestic appliance makers
Directeur sportif: Mike Neel
191, Andy Hampsten
192, Raúl Alcalá
193, Jonathan Boyer
*194, Jeff Bradley
195, Ron Kiefel
196, Dag-Otto Lauritzen
*197, Davis Phinney
198, Jeff Pierce
199, Bob Roll

ROLAND-SKALA-CHIORI (Belgium)
Sponsors: Piano makers and hi-fi firm
Directeur sportif: Roger Swerts
*201, Dietrich Thurau
*202, John Bogers
*203, Johan Capiot
204, Herman Frison
205, Rudy Patry
206, Jesper Skibby
207, Brian Sorensen
*208, Jac Van Der Poel
209, Patrick Verschueren

* Abandoned

SUPERMERCATI BRIANZOLI-CHÂTEAU D'AX (Italy)

Sponsors: Supermarket chain and wine makers

Directeur sportif: Gian-Luigi Stanga

*211, Vittorio Algeri

212, Stefano Allocchio

*213, Roberto Amadio

*214, Giovanni Bottoia

*215, Claudio Corti

*216, Stefano Guiliani

*217, Milan Jurco

*218, Dario Montani

219, Gerhard Zadrobilek

ANC-HALFORDS-LYCRA (Great Britain)

Sponsors: Haulage firm, cycle retailers

Directeurs sportifs: Ward Woutters and Phil Griffiths

221, Malcolm Elliott

*222, Bernard Chesneau

223, Guy Gallopin

*224, Graham Jones

225, Kvetoslav Palov

*226, Shane Sutton

*227, Steve Swart

228, Adrian Timmis

*229, Paul Watson

* Abandoned

WHO STAYED WHERE

DURING THE TOUR'S 25 DAYS, ANC-Halfords stayed in 20 different hotels, which varied in quality from an ancient college dormitory to a five-star hotel in Paris. For anyone wishing to follow in their footsteps, the overnight stops after each stage were:

Prologue, Stages 1 and 2, West Berlin: Novotel, Berlin Airport.
Stages 3 and 4: Hotel Sofitel, Stuttgart.
Stage 5: Hotel Ibis, Strasbourg.
Stage 6: Hôtel Émile Zola, Épinal.
Stage 7: Hôtel Climât de France, Romilly-sur-Seine.
Stage 8: Hôtel Fimotel, La Chapelle-Saint-Mesmin.
Stage 9: Hôtel Lac de Maine, Angers.
Stage 10: Hôtel Ibis, Poitiers South.
Stage 11: Hôtel au Bon Accueil, Tulle.
Stage 12: Hôtel Sofitel Aquitania, Bordeaux.
Stage 13: Hôtel Campanile, Pau.
Stage 14: Hôtel Adriatic, Lourdes.
Stage 15: Hôtel Mercure, Toulouse.

Stage 16: Collège Marcel Aymard, Millau.

Stages 17 and 18: Hôtel Climât de France, Avignon.

Stage 19: Guichard Immobilier, Villard-de-Lans.

Stage 20: Hôtel le Réfuge, L'Alpe d'Huez.

Stage 21: Résidence Aime 2000, La Plagne.

Stage 22: Résidence Locative, Avoriaz.

Stages 23 and 24: Hôtel Morot et Genève, Dijon.

Stage 25: Sofitel, Paris.